It Works for Me, Too!

D1244221

More Shared Tips for Effective Teaching

Hal Blythe
Foundation Professor of English
Eastern Kentucky University

Charlie Sweet
Foundation Professor of English
Eastern Kentucky University

NEW FORUMS PRESS, INC.
Stillwater, Oklahoma, U.S.A.

This book may be ordered in bulk quantities at discount from New Forums Press, Inc., P.O. Box 876, Stillwater, OK 74076 [Federal I.D. No. 73 1123239]. Printed in the United States of America.

International Standard Book Number: 1-58107-055-1

TABLE OF CONTENTS

INTRODUCTION vii

I. TEACHING PERSPECTIVES 1

A. Interrelating the Disciplines 2
B. Diversity 3
    1. Drawing Upon Personal Resources 3
    2. Walking in Another's Shoes 3
C. Group Learning 5
    1. Team Building in the Classroom 5
    2. CLEGS (Cooperative Learning
       Exchange Groups) 7
    3. Common Team Problems 8
    4. Making Group Discussions Work 10
    5. Partners in the Learning Process.................... 11
    6. Cooperative Learning 12
D. Microbursting 13
E. Rhythm and Hand Drumming 15
F. SWA (Selected Work Analysis) 16
G. Empathizing: Role-Playing in the Classroom 18
H. Professional Collegiality at
    Service in the Classroom 20
I. Duads 22
J. The Modified Socratic Method 23
K. ALFF (Active Learning Frequent Feedback)............... 23
L. "Daring" Teaching 25

II. PRACTICES AND POLICIES 27

A. Pre-course Class Preparation 28
    1. The Weekly Overview............................... 28
    2. Folders 28
    3. Multiple Outside Sources 29
    4. "We Will, We Will . . . Rock You" 30
B. First Day... 31
    1. Student Information 31
    2. E-Mail Instructions 31

3. Web Use 32
4. Previous Students as Visitors 32
5. Macaroni Art 32
6. Family Tree 33
7. Waste Not, Want Not 34

C. Testing and Quizzing 35
1. The Test 35
2. Quizzes 35
3. Bonus Round 36
4. Individual Quizzes 36
5. Quiz Bargaining 37
6. Group Testing 38
7. Collaborative Creative Quizzes 39
8. The Quote Selection Process 39
9. Posting Test Answers 40
10. Self-Posed Post-Test Questions 40
11. Makeups 41
12. Individual and Team
     Homework and Quizzes 41
13. Write Your Own Final 43

D. Class Organization 45
1. Previewing 45
2. All Good Things Must End—Effectively 45

E. Presentation Techniques 46
1. Demonstrations 46
2. Power Point 47
3. Props 47

F. Concerns 48
1. Block of Cheese Day 48
2. Children in the Classroom 49
3. Research 50
4. Your Mission: Not Impossible 50
5. Grading 51

G. Assessment 52
1. The End of Class Paragraph 52
2. Periodic Assessment 53
3. End of Class Questions 53

H. Syllabi and Information Sheets
    as Legal Documents 54

III. EXERCISES AND TECHNIQUES 57

A. Literature 58
    1. Their "Write" to Understand 58
    2. A Picture Is Worth... 59
    3. Engaging Students Through the Writings
       of Arthur Conan Doyle 60
    4. Visual Imagery in Discussing Literature 62
B. Writing 63
    1. A Swift Way to Spark Interest 63
    2. Real Writin' 64
    3. CLAD 65
    4. Supercharging Prose 66
    5. Teaching Voice in the Composition Classroom ... 68
    6. Teacher as Writing Role Model 68
C. PE 69
    1. Program Advocacy 69
    2. Mending the Fractured Physical
       Education Fairy Tale 71
D. Science: Molecular Biographies 73
E. Occupational Therapy 74
    1. Historical Contributors
       to Occupational Therapy 74
    2. Paper Dolls 74
    3. Making the Picture Complete 75
F. Library 76
    1. Where In the Library? 76
    2. What Don't You Like? 78
    3. Keyword Connection 79
    4. Boolean Basics 80
G. Cut-Across 81
    1. Framing Research 81
    2. *Jeopardy* 82
       a. Uniform Terminology *Jeopardy* 82
       b. Almost *Jeopardy* 82
       c. Game Shows in the Classroom 83
    3. Fun Team-Building Activities 84
       Initializers 84
       Communication Activities 85

        Low Level Activities 86
        High Level Activities 86
    4. Partner Projects 87
    5. Documenting Sources:
        A System Approach 88
    6. Blackboard Use 90
    7. SpongeBob SquarePants Lives........................ 90
    8. Performance Appraisal: Providing Feedback 91
    9. Motivation in the Work Place: Goal Setting 91
    10. Who Is a Leader? Why? 92
    11. Connecting Experience and Concept 92

AFTERWORD **95**

    1. Ten Timely Tips for Terrific Teaching 95

ACKNOWLEDGMENTS

We would like to thank Marsha Blythe, Melissa Norton, and Gail Hackworth. Without their hard work and patience, we never would have completed this project.

INTRODUCTION

Shaking his head one day last semester, Charlie came back to the office after observing a colleague's class as part of the department's new peer evaluation process. When Hal asked why he was puzzled, Charlie explained his surprise; after five classroom observations of five different instructors, he had discovered that no two colleagues' approaches to teaching were the same, yet each one was an effective teacher. Having been part of a college-wide mentoring program for the past twelve years, Hal admitted he too was constantly amazed at the variety of pedagogical practices he had observed. That moment got us both thinking about where we had left off our previous book on college teaching, *It Works For Me* (1998), with an "Afterword" on "Effective Teachers."

Gradually we began to realize that those fourteen traits (e.g. interactive, knowledgeable, enthusiastic) were fairly general, and what often made one of the classes we observed truly come alive was not a general overall teaching strategy, but a particular tactic (an exercise, an interchange, a special moment). Maybe, we reasoned, it was time for a sequel to our book, but instead of coming at effective teaching in generalities, abstractions, or by proceeding from day one to the final exam, we ought to concentrate on some of those little things effective teachers do somewhere during the 50 to 150 minutes allotted for each class.

In the four years since our first book on teaching, we have noticed both on our campus and around the country a new emphasis on the instructor as teacher (vs. scholar). We have read books on the subject, attended the prestigious Lilly Conference, helped establish a Teaching & Learning Center on our campus (Hal served as its first director), and written for new journals focusing on pedagogy, such as *Eureka Studies in Teaching Short Fiction*.

It Works For Me, Too! is our contribution to the Renaissance in College Pedagogy, our attempt to fuel this brightening interest in effective teaching. Like its predecessor, this book is a compilation of tips from workers in the collegiate trenches, but this time our contributors (some volunteers, some drafted) reflect the national interest in this subject and come from all around the country.

We begin with a few theoretical approaches, but the major focus of *IWFMT* (not exactly a memorable acronym) is that average day in the classroom and what momentary magic some instructor has injected into the mix to make the experience much more than average. Sometimes the advice is general, but usually it's specific. While the advisor may be in a different discipline than you, we have every confidence that you will be able to use this information in your area. After all, most of us weren't born good teachers – we made ourselves that.

During an observation last fall, Charlie watched as an instructor had her students reproduce exactly what Keats described on that famed Grecian urn. He went immediately into his Am Lit I class and had his students draw up the floor plan for the turret in which Poe's Lady Rowena is suddenly transformed into the lost love Ligeia. Only when his class could actually picture that pentagonal structure could they begin to see what magic might have transpired that fateful night.

The best tips aren't only shared; they are borrowed, reshaped, and adapted to one's own philosophy, and, as John D. MacDonald once said about good writing making more good readers, that reworking makes us all much better teachers.

So, read and adapt.

I. TEACHING PERSPECTIVES

Once upon a time the classroom experience consisted of a teacher (a/k/a The Sage on the Stage) standing inertly before a group of cowering students arranged in rigid, regimented rows listening to this god-like presence deliver from age-yellowed notes a fact-filled lecture that challenged the strongest hands attempting to transcribe the tomes of arcanna needed for regurgitation on the next exam. How times have changed!

Research in teaching and learning has revealed that while the time-honored lecture still has an important place in the classroom, today's students respond (many times more successfully) to a variety of approaches. Effective teachers are those who embrace this diversity, those who are willing to constantly try new things. Sometimes this risk-taking involves a specific technique or exercise (covered in later sections of this book); sometimes it involves taking an entirely different approach to the classroom experience.

The "tips" offered in this section let you sample a few different perspectives on just what it is that can occur in a classroom and how a slight variation in your approach to the teacher-student, student-student, teacher-material, or student-material relationship might reap huge dividends in your classes. The approaches are by no means exhaustive, but each one is stimulating.

Here's hoping one or more will even lead you to your own new way of reinventing the classroom experience.

INTERRELATING THE DISCIPLINES
Robert L. Burns

Sometimes in class we focus on a single tree when students also need to see the forest.

It is important that you help your students make connections between the academic discipline and content you are teaching this term and the others they face in a balanced curriculum. Formal interdisciplinary programs and team teaching are not the only ways to enrich your classes toward an "interrelation of the disciplines."

Teaching a piece of literature, an historical event, or an economic theory as if its importance were isolated within your class not only shortchanges students but limits the variety of teaching methods open to you. Instead, explain how the novel you are teaching not only reflects a history but may have influenced it. Blake's songs are easier to understand when you pair them with the socio-political and economic environment of the time.

Using the "literary period" to help understand the literature is perhaps the most common of interdisciplinary approaches. But don't forgo using the reverse technique. Teaching economic theory, education, or physics? Include what thinkers were reading at the time and how it influenced them. Regardless of the academic discipline you teach, it is unlikely that its leading figures, theories, or developments could have happened in isolation from the lives being led every day—the literature, music, art, philosophy, politics, religion, and science. Use it all.

DIVERSITY

DRAWING UPON PERSONAL RESOURCES
Robert L. Burns

Polonious wasn't always a fool—like the time he advised young Hamlet, "To thine own self be true."

It looks like the federal courts are going to be busy with the questions of how schools can improve diversity through admissions. Recent decisions, sure to be appealed on up the legal system, are starting to expand the definition of diversity so that it cannot be simply a matter of race. While the arguments continue in the courts, you can bring a rich diversity into your classroom every day.

Regardless of your race, don't overlook the powerful educational value of exposing your students to characteristics you bring into the room because of your personal background and personality. Your way of speaking, for example, including regional accent and vocabulary, can be an element that helps students learn to work with and to value diverse backgrounds. Your life's experiences as a child, during your own college days, or at lunch last week can enrich students' understanding of what life is like for other people. Most of them, so far, are fairly limited in their own experiences.

Keep in mind that the class you are teaching is not "Me 101," and save the graduate-school war stories for coffee time with colleagues who can defend themselves with similar volleys of their own. But be yourself in the classroom, with all of your "regionalisms." We all get enough pasteurization from the mass media, and you can help students realize that we are more mosaic than melting pot.

WALKING IN ANOTHER'S SHOES
Lisa M. Vaughn, Brenau University

Still, Grasshopper, each tree in the forest is unique.

When teaching about diversity and cultural differences, instructors typically utilize two predominant approaches. One approach is what I call the "World's Fair/Epcot Center" approach where the emphasis is on the food, customs, holidays, and dress of a particular cultural group. Another approach that is common in cross-cultural psychology is one that involves contrasting and comparing numerous constructs across cultural groups (e.g., relationships, religion, sexuality, personality, healthcare practices, etc.). The World's Fair approach helps students to be exposed to practices and people who are different from their own backgrounds, and the cross-cultural psychology approach helps students to gain a more in-depth understanding of similarities and differences across cultures as well as the underlying frameworks for discrimination, prejudice, and oppression.

After making a decision about which overarching approach (World's Fair, cross-cultural psychology, or a combination of the two), I attempt to emphasize several important ideas through a variety of assignments and work both in-class and out-of-class:

- "Cultural identity" is not just about race and ethnicity. It also involves a complex interaction of gender, class, sexual orientation, disability, religion, geography, and family background.
- We all have a deeply rooted "cultural identity" that is the essence of who we are.
- Walking in another's shoes is essential to begin to understand the experience of discrimination, oppression, and prejudice. This task is accomplished through reading about, talking and interacting with, and experiencing firsthand as many people from other cultural groups as possible.
- Understanding the "other" and what it means to be ignored or overlooked can lead to insights about our own acts of disregarding and overlooking others. Most of us have been in the position of both oppressor and oppressed.
- Any type of oppression is essentially destructive and hurtful, and we must resist the urge to engage in what Elizabeth Martinez calls "oppression Olympics" where minority groups compete for status of most oppressed.
- Many of our deeply held convictions, beliefs, traditions, and customs are simply social constructions within our society. Examining the social constructions of different cultures often highlights our own ethnocentrism.
- Recognizing our own prejudices and tendencies to stereotype can be painful and challenging, causing us to be defensive about our own cultural identity.

I also use a number of general teaching methods that I believe enhance the learning of diversity issues:

- In general, get students out of their comfort zone—not totally overwhelmed but challenged. Remember that optimal learning involves some tension and discomfort. Students can feel motivated to learn if they are challenged to think outside their normal frameworks.

- Have students talk to and interview people from different cultural backgrounds. This task can occur in class with other students and through assignments that require interviews with people outside of class.
- Emphasize experiential and active learning activities (e.g., writing, field experiences, reflection, literature searches, internet searches, critical thinking questions, and varied intercultural immersion experiences, etc.).
- Provide and require exposure opportunities where students can experience different cultures first-hand.
- Cultivate a positive learning environment where class participation is encouraged so that students can express thoughts, opinions, and perspectives about challenging issues.
- Allow students to express their creativity and personal interests (e.g., posters about specific cultural groups or cultural issues, experiential and fun experiences/assignments outside of classroom, etc.).
- Use lots of variety in teaching methods, teaching styles, and teaching resources to continually stimulate student interest.

GROUP LEARNING

TEAM BUILDING IN THE CLASSROOM
Heather Hall, Elmhurst College

All right, so maybe we didn't learn everything we had to know in kindergarten. Back on the elementary school playground (or grade school for us oldies), it was always more fun playing tag or dodgeball (that most violent of games) when you chose up teams.

Team building is fun, important, and is gaining momentum! Team building offers not only an opportunity to increase the self-esteem of the participants and to better the relationship among team or group members, but it also adds an appreciation of the diversity of skills people bring to a group.

Team-building activities develop specific skills in communication, decision making, conflict resolution, risk-taking, and affirmation.

Teamwork promotes cooperation and cohesiveness over competition, in which everyone contributes a part to make a stronger whole.

Through team-building activities, individuals are able to build character through competition with themselves and cooperation with others.

Team-building activities can provide the moral growth that facilitates group cohesion and enthusiasm for one's class.

Starting the school year or semester with team-building activities sets a positive atmosphere that carries over to later units of study.

If you decide to try team-building activities, a couple of ways exist to present the challenges. One method is to set up the same challenge for all groups. A second method is to set up several challenges and let the groups rotate. Which of these methods you decide to use would more than likely depend on the physical space that you have available and the size of your group. In the classroom, I set up one challenge and all of the groups work on the same challenge.

If you decide to try team-building activities, some things you should keep in mind as a facilitator, classroom teacher or coach:

1. It is extremely important from the start to discourage negative pressure and put-downs. It is important to stress to your group members that even a frown, impatient look, or rolling of the eyes can send negative messages and put undue pressure on a fellow group member.
2. Along these same lines, you should encourage praise. Every one of us likes to know when our efforts are appreciated and recognized. This time is very difficult for some individuals because they are not accustomed to praising classmates. In order to encourage praise, you should set the example and use praise phrases appropriately whenever your group members are working on challenges.
3. The teacher or coach should *assign* members to the teams. For most of the activities, groups of 8-10 work best.
4. As a facilitator, you also need to avoid solving the challenges for your students. It's o.k. for them to struggle.
5. If a team does not finish a challenge, consider letting them continue with it the next class period. I have found it is important for groups to follow through, complete their tasks, and fight through frustration and time contraints.
6. In addition, as a facilitator, you also have to be aware of liability issues.

The activities I use are not high-element challenges that require a waiver form or parental consent; however, there are certain common sense quidelines to follow. The best way to remember these is with the acronym PEEP. PEEP stands for personal, environmental, emotional, and physical safety.

- P - Personal safety requires each participant to have proper clothing and footwear. Items such as belts and jewelry should not be allowed.
- E - Environmental safety requires that the area be clear of debris or obstacles that could cause injury before starting the activities.
- E – Emotional safety is mindful of the fact that challenge should be by choice.
- P – Physical safety. As a facilitator, do not allow the participants in physical activities to do something that you know is not safe (for example, standing on someone's shoulders, standing in the middle of someone's back who is on all fours, throwing bodies through the air, etc.). Remind participants to always protect the head of group members.

COOPERATIVE LEARNING EXCHANGE GROUPS (CLEGS) WITH SALON EXCHANGES
Lisa M. Vaughn, Brenau University

Remember sitting around the fraternity/sorority house tapping KEGS. Oh, this is CLEGS—nevermind!

The Cooperative Learning and Exchange Group (CLEG) with salon exchanges is a structured small group out-of-class requirement in some of my classes.

Students are assigned to their CLEG during the first class (usually 3-5 students per CLEG). The CLEGS are required to meet once a week, and students in each CLEG can structure the group however they want. I do give them guidelines and suggestions for making the group run smoothly (e.g., developing ground rules, doing some ice breakers and teambuilding as a group, rotating facilitation, etc.). Each week, the CLEGS have to do particular assignments, such as completing group quizzes on-line, discussing reading for that week, completing an assignment/activity/worksheet within the group, summarizing the readings, answering critical thinking questions, etc. Each week it is mandatory that the CLEG have a "salon exchange" where they come together either in person or on-line to discuss the themes and ideas generated from that week in class or through the assignments. After the "salon exchange," each CLEG is required to submit a summary of their discussion to me.

Each CLEG is told that they should monitor individual group members to ensure that each person is keeping up with his/her assignments. At midterm and at the end of the semester, each member of each CLEG is asked to give a peer assessment of each individual within their group. They are told that the assessment should take into account each individual's weekly participation and work regarding the salon exchanges and any assignments.

Some reasons for the success of the CLEGS:

- Students are allowed to process/discuss/communicate together without a teacher.
- Students are engaged in peer learning, which is often as powerful as teacher-student learning.
- Students are applying information learned in the class and through readings.
- Students learn how to rely on others in the group.
- The groups are continuous and provide constancy with weekly meetings.
- Students learn how to build community and resolve issues as they arise in the group.
- I am available as a consultant to any of the groups in case things get too difficult.
- Because the CLEGS have to provide a peer assessment, they tend to be accountable and reliable to each other throughout the semester.

COMMON TEAM PROBLEMS
Wallace R. Wood, University of Cincinnati

When teams don't hit on all eight cylinders, good coaches make adjustments.

Working in groups can be highly beneficial, but such "teamwork" can present problems. Here are some actions to be taken to resolve these problems.

Floundering
- Review missions and make sure they are clear to everyone
- Get the group to look critically at how the meeting is run
- Cross-check problem-solving steps
- Get help from facilitator
- Check whether everyone is honest and objective

Unquestioned Acceptance of Opinions as Facts
- Question whether opinion or fact…ask for data

Rush to Accomplishment
- Confront rushers; make sure team did not skip problem-solving steps
- Make sure he/she has no other selfish interests

Attribution (question the experts and listen to everyone)
- Don't discount any team member for expertise or lack of expertise
- Ask for data and facts; consider brainstorming
- Call in an expert

Irrelevant Statements or Ones that Fall Flat
- Every statement may have two meanings. . .ask the speaker what he/she meant
- Some people are philosophical…identify them early
- Discuss the subject off-line with person

Wanderlust: Digression and Tangents
- Most people have a natural tendency to stray from topic
- Refer to a written agenda
- Question whether the conversation relates to the topic
- Bluntly state, "We are not on track"

"No Shows"
- Cancel the meeting if key players or more than two members are missing
- Address issue in very next meeting
- Question meeting time
- Select a member to issue minutes and inform facilitator

Changes in Team Membership
- Do not spend time bringing a new member on board
- Get someone to take action item to bring new member up to speed

MAKING GROUP DISCUSSIONS WORK

Robin K. Morgan, Indiana University Southeast

Research loves collaborative learning, but good group discussions are like Hemingway's iceberg—there's a lot beneath the surface. Or, as John Wooden, the Wizard of Westwood, said, "Failing to prepare is preparing to fail."

I have been using some variation of group discussions since I began teaching in 1982. In the beginning, some group discussions worked well and some, well, …bombed!

In the intervening years, I have developed a collection of principles for ensuring relatively successful and productive group discussions. I'd like to share these basic principles here.

Composition: Let me be blunt. I stack the groups to ensure success. First, I have found that group size is critical. Groups need to be large enough to ensure discussion but not so large that individuals lose a sense of responsibility for making sure that discussion is successful. I find group size of 4-6 most successful. Second, I do not assign any group activity until after the first 2-3 weeks of class. During this initial period, I observe class dynamics and the behavior of individual students. I then construct groups that have a balance of student abilities. Each group needs to have someone willing to initiate discussion. In addition, it is important that the weaker students be balanced across groups. Personality conflicts among students may also be "controlled" by careful group placement.

Preparation: Both the students and the instructor must engage in preparation in order to have successful group discussions. The instructor must carefully select reading material that challenges the students to consider issues. If the reading presents only one perspective, the group discussion will be minimal. Second, the instructor must prepare questions for the students to answer prior to coming to the group discussion. These questions must guide the students into a discussion but not limit the students' thinking. On the day of the discussion, students must have completed the reading and the pre-discussion questions in order to participate in the discussion. At first, I worried that students would not complete the questions. This worry did not happen due to factors I'll explain under "grading." Finally, students must be given the opportunity to write additional information on their sheets as a result of group discussion. This step helps to focus the group discussion on the topic and reduces extraneous, unrelated discussions such as the latest movie.

Grading: Yes, I grade group discussions. I have found that students will expend energy on an assignment proportional to how many points that assignment is worth in relation to their final grade. Given this truth, group discussions (I typically have 5-6 group discussions over a semester) are never worth less than a third of their total grade. I require students to submit their pre-discussion question form at the end of the discussion. Prior to the discussion they may answer the questions in ink (or typing). They may add information during the discussion, but only in pencil. Their grade is then based on the combination of their pre-discussion efforts and their additions during discussion. Students seem to like the fact that their individual efforts are being recognized. In addition, they recognize that an effective group discussion can help their grade. As the instructor, I read and comment on each student's paper. Suggestions for improvement are recorded and subsequent papers are checked to see if that improvement has occurred. Students frequently relay their amazement that I have actually read their papers, leading me to the conclusion that instructors should seriously consider the value of ungraded (or unread) assignments.

Instructor's Role During Discussions: Once the discussion begins, I wander the room listening in on the discussions. Rarely do I comment. My only comments might be to ask a question to stimulate discussion of a point the group may not have considered. Group discussions work best in my classes if I create the environment conducive to such discussions, then get out of the students' way. This was difficult at first because I was accustomed to directing the students. However, staying out of their way has led to the students developing ideas I had not considered.

Concluding Discussions: In my experience it is critical to save 15-20 minutes at the end of class for students to select a group spokesperson to report back to the class. Members of other groups may ask questions leading to excellent full-class discussions. In addition, this final period allows the instructor to correct any inaccurate conclusions groups may have reached.

PARTNERS IN THE LEARNING PROCESS
Pat Calie, Eastern Kentucky University

More help for that playground we now call the classroom.

One strategy that I really try to work at is effectively engaging students in the learning process. I repeatedly tell students that learning is a participant sport, not a spectator sport. And, in my experience, the majority of students appreciate the opportunity to assume some control of the learning process.

One approach that I use covers several aspects of effective teaching: student participation, starting the class session in an effective manner, developing teamwork and team skills among students, and student empowerment.

I teach genetics, and emphasize a "problem-solving," analytical approach. I assign a number of examples/experimental analyses for homework and review selected representative examples during class time. I ask my students to form teams of 4 students each, and I assign each team the responsibility of reviewing a selected problem for us at the beginning of each class. In class, while the team is writing their solution and reasoning on the board, I will review the problem orally and comment on particular approaches to arrive at the correct solution. I then turn over the class to the team of students, who take us through the analysis and correct solution to a problem or analysis of a genetic experiment. I will help the team if they need assistance, but after the first week or two the students are often able to demonstrate the correct solution without my input.

Students have regularly commented on their appreciation of being allowed to be active participants in the learning process. And I find that often the students' explanations of a particular solution are clearer and more logical to their fellow students than mine are! Perhaps the most rewarding aspect of this process is watching students' confidence grow, as they realize that they can master the material well enough to teach a portion of it to their peers. And being one of a team of four at the front of a class is much less intimidating than being the only person standing.

COOPERATIVE LEARNING
Kenneth Clawson, Eastern Kentucky University

Four/For Students

I place students in all my classes in small (usually 4 students) learning groups. I use these groups in a variety of ways. One example is to assign topics or sections of a chapter to each group. They are to discuss it and then present or lead the discussion on this topic with the whole class. I feel this technique is especially effective in preparing pre-service teachers. Of course, it also works well with my graduate students, most of whom are teachers, counselors, etc.

MICROBURSTING
Lisa Vaughn, Brenau University

Why settle for one dish when there's a smorgasbord of approaches out there?

Do you teach in the same way you were taught? Do you teach "yourself," reflecting how you prefer to learn? Amidst the shuffle of professional commitments and the rapidly increasing amount of new information plus the constant changes in academic disciplines, professors tend to rely on one of these two strategies for teaching. College teaching itself tends to remain traditional despite the change occurring in academics.

In addition, many professors have had little formal training in educational theories and techniques. At the same time, professors are subject to increasing demands on their time for other activities, such as grant writing and research. The result is a decrease in the actual amount of time available for teaching and the concomitant need for increased efficiency during that limited teaching time. There is a need for a teaching-learning model that is exciting, fun, and motivating for both teacher and learner and that maximizes the learning process during this time of training and education.

Microburst Teaching and Learning is a strategy for combining various teaching styles and methods to interest and motivate students with different and sometimes disparate learning styles for the ultimate purpose of enhancing and strengthening the learning process. Microburst teaching utilizes different teaching methods and teaching styles that are interchanged and presented in brief "bursts" of time. The label "microburst" comes from a meteorological term meaning "an intense, short-lived localized event occurring during a rain storm."

Learners have preferred learning styles that are based on past learning experiences, teaching styles to which they have been exposed, and their own strengths and optimal methods of receiving, processing, storing, and expressing information. These preferred styles can change over time, especially upon exposure to changing teaching styles, but change requires effort and work. As in all aspects of teaching and learning, some learners have innate learning skills that allow for considerable adaptability and can utilize many styles with ease. Others tend to be locked into a predominant style and have difficulty with the learning process when exposed to new teaching methods.

One of the marks of a good teacher is the ability to stretch the learner's learning style and increase the breadth of learning abilities. By using a variety of teaching methods and styles, teachers can expose learners to both familiar and unfamiliar ways of learning without designating any individual as "different." This provides both tension and comfort during the process, which encourages adaptability to multiple learning styles and encourages lifelong learning. An added bonus to this model is that learners have greater opportunity to excel if their dominant (preferred) and less dominant learning styles are addressed in the learning process. For example, if a learner is not a good test taker, then she/he can demonstrate her/his knowledge in discussion or activities.

The Microburst Model requires knowledge and experience with a variety of teaching methods. Some variations in teaching methods are simple and may appear intuitive. However, making them explicit increases the likelihood that they will be used. Some professors complain that they don't know about other teaching methods besides the "tried and true" lecture and small group discussion. By having a repertoire of teaching methods in the teacher's "bag of tricks," teachers will have the necessary tools to begin to stretch their own teaching styles while at the same time stretching their learners' learning styles. Certain methods will be more applicable to particular settings (e.g., the large classroom versus small seminar class), and some are more appropriate to certain size groups. For instance, in a large lecture class, instead of presenting Chapter X as the sage on the stage, an instructor might provide a mini-background lecture, having the class divide into 5 groups so that each group can solve one of Chapter X's study questions, giving all students a hands-on handout, and finally assigning a website they all have to check.

Balancing academic productivity with time for effective teaching remains a central concern in most academic settings. Because every university setting has unique and complex demands, professors need a variety of options to carry out the teaching-learning process in a manner that best fits their own setting. The Microburst Model suggests multiple tools for the busy teacher to maximize the limited opportunities for teaching and learning. If professors recognize that at any "teachable moment," there are several possibilities of connecting with the learner, rather than just one or two traditional teaching methods, perhaps the freedom to choose among multiple techniques will optimize not only the teacher's time, productivity, and teaching motivation, but maximize the learning of the student.

(An earlier version of this piece appeared in *Medical Teacher.*)

RHYTHM AND HAND DRUMMING
Lisa M. Vaughn, Brenau University
Paula Bickham, Eastern Kentucky University

Just when you think you've heard every possible teamwork strategy, something new (that's really quite old) comes along. Teaching, like existence itself, is ever evolving. Lisa and Paula suggest here an activity that at first sounds like it's confined to Music Departments. On review, you'll see that this technique could be utilized by any discipline wishing to teach teamwork and unity.

Rhythm and hand drumming have been used in a variety of settings for numerous purposes, including spirit building among personal growth/religious groups, team building in organizations and corporations, tension breakers with groups in conflict, cohesiveness at large conferences, and building community in grass roots organizations. In general, percussive rhythm and hand drumming have many noted and researched benefits, including positive physiological effects such as enhancement of cognitive and motor skills; creative self-expression; collaboration among diverse groups of people; personal healing; participative and peaceful community building; expression of culture; enhancement of interpersonal skills such as listening, collaboration, communication, and teamwork; and fun/enjoyment.

Rhythm and hand drumming can benefit the teaching/learning process in several ways:

- **Creativity/freedom of expression**: It is important to establish that each person has a unique voice to contribute to the group early on, as this encourages listening to others and hearing one's own voice in relationship to the group.
- **Different sensory experience**: Integrating sensory experiences in higher education can create flexibility in learning styles. Not everyone perceives the interrelationship between patterns of light and color (visual), numerical patterns (cerebral), tonal and rhythmical patterns (audio), or movement and touch (kinetic). Sensory experience can form the basis for a sense of self and meaning to occur. This aspect is important in the learning cycle as students become more active in making connections and experiencing discovery.
- **Cohesion/collaboration/cooperation/teamwork/unity**: Unlike other forms of group experience, the drum/rhythm circle quickly forms a sense of cohe-

sion as all participants come together to create a common voice. There is a sense of aliveness and vitality that is unique to these types of experiences as group participants are focused on here-and-now interactions.

- **Fun/"break the ice":** Rhythm and drumming can ease tensions, especially when a group first forms. As in any physical activity performed in a classroom setting where people are normally expecting to engage the mind only and "check the body at the door," rhythm and drumming activities can help bridge the mind-body gap, which can be an artificial and quite unnecessary barrier that diminishes the full potential of both teaching and learning.

- **Teacher insight and awareness**: Rhythm and drumming can help teachers to become more aware of themselves, students, and the group-as-a-whole. Rhythm and drumming act as "masks" for the personality to flow through, inviting spontaneous interactions. The group becomes the teacher rather than a single person disseminating information, increasing opportunities for new connections and discoveries to be made.

- **Therapeutic aspects** (for counseling, health-related disciplines): Drumming has been used with schizophrenic and Alzheimer's patients as well as for counseling purposes with adults, teenagers, and children. It is a vehicle to teach basic communication skills such as listening, trust, how to give and receive feedback without judgement, and how to express a unique voice while being a part of the group. Coming together as one voice to achieve a common goal provides members with a sense of purpose, success in collaboration, and can open new ways to encounter others and heal past emotional scars.

SWA (SELECTED WORKS ANALYSIS)
Ginny Hencken Elsasser, Centenary College

Remember how good you felt in the old school lunchroom when you had chocolate milk while everybody else was drinking plain white? Here's an approach that allows for student individualism in the midst of necessary classroom conformity and can be used in English, History and Sociology classes as well as those Ginny suggests.

The Selected Works Analysis (SWA) is a creative and innovative strategy for improving the teaching and learning process. It is a valuable alternative to the traditional test format for evaluating student learning and is useful for a wide variety of content areas. It does require high levels of critical thinking and may be more appropriate for upper-level courses. The purpose/objective is to encourage students to become actively engaged in the analysis, integration, and appreciation of course content. This strategy provides an opportunity for the student to study and analyze a selected work or body of work for a semester. This assignment was first conducted with a senior-level class in the Social and Psychological Aspects of Clothing during the Spring 1999 semester and repeated in Spring 2000 and 2001. The assigned text was *The Social Psychology of Clothing* by Susan Kaiser. As the content of each section of the book is covered, the students relate a relevant passage or concept from each chapter to their selected work. A written paper and an oral presentation about the material are required.

Each student selects an appropriate work or body of work at the beginning of the semester. Students are advised to select a work very carefully to ensure that it can be used for the entire semester. Student selections have included: *The Bible, The Golden Girls, Pretty Woman,* Madonna, Versace, Valentino, *The Indiana Jones Trilogy, Clueless, The Last Emperor, Fight Club,* and *General Hospital.*

Instead of traditional tests, students prepare oral reports and written papers that document how their selected work relates to the content of the chapter. During the presentation the student is required to initiate discussion about their conclusions. Specific citations from the chapter and from the selected work are required. Citations from the work may be visual (video clips, slides, photographs, images from the Internet or books).

Interviews with students indicate that they like the assignment and think they are learning more than if they were being tested in a traditional format. Student comments included: "With the SWA I have to really read the chapter and think about what it says"; "I never really read a textbook before this assignment"; "I have to understand it and relate it to my selected work instead of just studying the chapter and then forgetting it after the test"; "I am learning as much from the other presentations as I am from analyzing my own selected work." Student response to SWA has been very positive and the strategy will be continued.

Students should present an introduction to their selected work to "set the stage" for the analysis. The instructor may need to impose time limits on presentations. Some students need to be encouraged to do more in-depth analysis. Some students may just list a work reference and then a chapter reference without the required integration and analysis. To ensure a variety of topics, each student should choose a different selected work. For large classes students can work in groups, and/or the presentations can rotate while written papers are submitted for each chapter or section of the text. SWA could be adapted for use in Retailing, Marketing, Fundamentals of Design, or Introduction to Fashion classes.

EMPATHIZING: ROLE-PLAYING IN THE CLASSROOM

Hal Blythe and Charlie Sweet, Eastern Kentucky University

Do these guys need an intro?

One day in the midst of discussing a classic work with his World Lit students, Hal looked out at the class and almost visibly recoiled. He was suddenly struck by a horrifying image: the students were staring at Dante's *Inferno* as though it were a dusty old tome that should not be removed from a library shelf except under penalty of death, or at least banishment to one of Dante's circles of hell.

The lit that he so loved and enthusiastically lived with each day reached his students stillborn.

Afterwards, we skull-sessioned on something we could do to make the lit come alive. Somewhere in our discussion it struck us that these were students reared not in nurseries, but cineplexes and family rooms with wide-screen projection TV's. What they seemed to like most were stories in which they could participate.

To get them to empathize with literary characters, we started by making them "characters." No, we didn't, as some of our colleagues do in classes like Shakespeare and Modern Drama, assign them roles in the play and have them read and act out the lines (though this method is highly effective in places). Many of our works were poems or stories without much dialogue, so we had our students become one of the characters in those works.

Let us show you how this role-playing works. Charlie was getting ready to teach "My Last Duchess." He assigned his students a different way to read Browning's poem. "You are not readers," he instructed the class. "In fact, you are a servant for Italy's famous Count Gismond. He has given you a new duty. Today you are to ride over to Duke Ferrara's ancestral home. The Duke through a previous arrangement is marrying the Count's daughter, and you must finalize the wedding arrangements, especially the matter of the dowry. When you return, tell the Count what you think of the daughter's new husband."

The next period when the students arrived, Charlie told them, "My name is

Count Gismond, and if you wish to stay in my employ, you will tell me the absolute truth about the character of my new son-in-law, Duke Ferrara." Charlie then went around the room asking his various "servants" for their impression of Ferrara. The result was an enjoyable class period in which literature truly came alive.

Should you try this approach all the time? Of course not. For one thing some works don't lend themselves to role-playing (think Castiglione or "The Art of Fiction"). Moreover, role-playing provides variety and a change of pace; role-playing every day could lead to a "Been there, done that" reaction from the class.

But try the exercise some time. Students could be parishioners walking into Browning St. Praxed's Church and overhearing their bishop's dying words. Make the class into a coroner's jury and let them hear the testimony of George Tesman and Thea Elvsted as to why Hedda Gabler took her own life (hint: don't let Judge Brack preside). Let students become daily workers in Tilbury Town wondering why Richard Cory committed suicide. How about playing *Baywatch 1890* wherein your students are lifeguards watching an open boat on the horizon. Do those rowers need rescuing, or are they out there for a six-hour cruise? "You are touring the Shiloh battlefield and you see a young woman in the distance on a bluff overlooking the Tennessee River moving her arms. What in the name of Bobbie Ann Mason does she want?"

While we use this approach in our English classes, we see no reason it couldn't be applied to other disciplines. Why can't art students become Whistlers and Picassos to explain what they were trying to get across in picture x.? Can't history students become opposing generals, dueling orators, Franklin and Jefferson arguing over whether to include an anti-slavery clause in the Declaration of Independence?

Ultimately, such role-playing does even more than offer variety or make the literary work come alive. When students are forced to act, to become a character, they learn to empathize, and from that point on every time they read they find themselves more open, more willing to go with the flow and identify with the characters.

PROFESSIONAL COLLEGIALITY AT SERVICE IN THE CLASSROOM

Paula Kopacz, Eastern Kentucky University

If Will Rogers had taught in academia, he might have written the following piece. Sometimes our greatest assets are all around us, and once we recognize the worth of our colleagues, many good things can happen.

Awash in today's criticism of higher education and stressed with the burdens of underprepared students and overscheduled committee meetings, we should remember that one of the biggest—and perhaps most overlooked—perks of our profession is the casual development of long-term professional relationships. With corporate loyalty the fossil of a by-gone generation, academia is one of the few remaining professions that give employees the luxury of staying with a given employer for an extended period of years. Indeed, even the customary seven probationary years before tenure seem an eternity to people in other professions, where advancement generally means relocation, and relocation means new professional relationships. Yet not only is the personal value of academics' extended relationships frequently underappreciated, but their potential for enhancing the classroom experience and the learning process is also neglected. Those of us fortunate enough to find ourselves with a given set of colleagues for decades should begin to look to the benefits of our situation, and use our relationships to enhance the classroom experience for our students. Here is how it has developed, albeit serendipitously, for me.

Because our department is quite large, several of us have overlapping fields of interest. Through interaction on committees and presentations at conferences and college symposia, through the normal process of peer evaluation over the years, alternating evaluator and evaluated, one of my colleagues and I have found out a good deal about each other's professional interests, biases, and slants. Beyond our shared interest in nineteenth-century American Literature, we found many differences and much to disagree about. When teaching the traditional canon, his course focuses on Gothic Literature; mine looks at writers with Puritan roots. When he goes outside the traditional canon, he searches for popular writers in popular culture; I look at women writers. He prefers works in the later margins of the period; I prefer works in the early part of the period. And so it goes.

In some cases this situation could be a source of academic tension and professional rivalry, but over the years, we have learned both to appreciate the other's perspective and to use it to enhance our students' understanding. For one thing, we have sat in on each other's classes. Sometimes this visit has been for formal evaluation, but at other times, one or the other just popped in unexpectedly for fun. One memorable instance occurred during a semester when we found that a significant group of students was taking courses from both of us. After a period of asking the students what went on in the other's class, my colleague walked by my class one day and asked if he could join. He sat down right next to me, and as I spoke and as my students' spoke, we solicited his opinion. For me, it was interesting to hear the opinion of someone else in my field there to address at the moment what I was saying both in its context and in its detail. Nothing was on the line. We were just a couple of people who love what they teach talking about it in front of and with students, most of whom were known to both of us. The situation was spontaneous, unplanned, and fun and exciting for both of us, and for the students as well, who learned not only how academics *talk to each other* about the material they love, but also about professional discourse in the field.

Granted, this situation could not have happened without years of preparation, as it were—not quite the cosmic evolution Whitman describes when he says "All forces have been steadily employ'd to complete. . .me" (l. 1167, "Song of Myself"), but years of casually getting to know each other well—years of being colleagues—exactly the situation most academics fail to recognize as the boon it is. And granted, we don't often have the *time* to spend an extra hour in a colleague's class just for the fun of it. But my colleague and I spice up our classes even without spending *extra* time. We do it by bringing our different professional perspectives out into the open in our classes. I have asked students, for instance, when they respond to my question in a certain way, if they got that viewpoint from my colleague. If they respond positively, I might say, "Well, you go and tell Dr. ____ that ____, and see what he says to that." In the next class, I'll ask the student for his account of Dr. ____'s answer. And so students become go-betweens in an ongoing debate. They find it exciting and fun—but also non-threatening because they are merely *reporting* my colleague's answer, and not personally responsible for debating with me. Those who are in my colleague's class obviously have to take his perspectives and opinions seriously, and they have to take mine seriously as well. So while they do not have to debate me in public, they do have to think for themselves. The tone of our public professional debate is light-hearted. Sometimes, when we teach in the same classroom, we leave "notes" for each other, pushing each other's buttons, as it were, as when I write on the blackboard, "Emily Dickinson is the greatest American poet ever." My students and I can't wait to walk into our next class to see how my colleague responded to my red flag.

Perhaps we need a few words of caution: involving students in our light-hearted public debate has worked for us in upper-division courses, English courses taken by sophomores, juniors, and seniors, most of whom are English majors or English-Education majors. My experience team teaching a freshman course suggests our strategy would not work with lower-division courses. In team-teaching a first semester freshman Honors course with a colleague from the Philosophy department one year, we deliberately tried to emphasize the different perspectives of a philosopher and a literary critic. Instead of involving students, however, our ploy distanced them. They fell silent. They took the attitude that they would wait until we had figured it out and agreed on the "answer," and then they would learn it and spew it back to us. They were too inexperienced to understand or appreciate the nature of intellectual discourse. The students need a modest degree of intellectual and academic maturity and training in the humanities to enjoy dialogue between professors. They need some training in how to appreciate intellectual debate. Our interclassroom public discussion helps them learn this important intellectual habit. Then, too, it goes without saying that the professors themselves must genuinely respect each other's views and must have a good sense of camaraderie in order to play the game.

But I suspect those of us who have worked together for many long years have developed more of these relationships than we recognize. The light-hearted academic bickering and banter have made professional growth possible and the workplace environment certainly more palatable. Probably many of us have done this among ourselves for years. This result is academic collegiality—it's why we chose our profession. My point is that we need to share the benefits of long academic life with our students to enrich and energize the classroom experience for all of us. There *is* a benefit to tenure, to long-term academic relationships. Let's make the most of them!

DUADS
Bruce Davis, Eastern Kentucky University

Duads are better than one (head).

For any type of class, whether hands-on, skills-oriented or the standard content-oriented class, I let students work together on activities and assignments. This is real-world practice and there is usually a synergy for learning when two people are involved on a particular problem. However, I try to keep the team to two students; more creates problems and inequities in contribution. Sometimes three are ok by special permission, but more than that is an unacceptable mob. I'm still traditional with tests, with each person responsible for his/her own work. I've tried team testing, but the process is more like an activity than a test.

THE MODIFIED SOCRATIC METHOD
Bruce Davis, Eastern Kentucky University

A sage on the stage without a page could become the rage.

I seldom lecture any more but prefer to engage the class in discussion of the topic at hand. I post my notes (often in question form) on the course web page, require that students prepare for class from them and the assigned reading, and then come to class ready to answer questions and address the class notes. I initially use a modified Socratic method, which is really more of a discussion rather than a grilling for answers. We try to make the topic relevant rather than simply coverage, e.g., making it meaningful to student lives and the real world. Everyone is included frequently, and I call on students as much as I accept raised hands. We keep the discussion fun, but productive. A light touch with the students is needed, e.g., jokes, no strong admonishments, etc. This method helps to keep the class attentive and focused. The down-side is lack of as much preparation as I would prefer, and too often students rely upon native intelligence rather than learned knowledge. The relative few points for participation aren't convincing enough for some students, but I continue to work on this aspect. However imperfect, this approach is much more acceptable and effective than pure lecture.

ALFF (ACTIVE LEARNING FREQUENT FEEDBACK)
Wallace R. Wood, University of Cincinnati

ALFF is not that loveable TV sitcom E.T. but a coordinated system of teaching. Here's an information sheet Wally hands out at the beginning of the semester.

Active Learning Frequent Feedback (ALFF) is a coordinated set of teaching methods based on the premise that involvement increases depth and quality of learning and increases retention of learning. ALFF Strategy has three parts: Tailored Teaching, Writing-to-Learn, and Collaborative Learning.

Tailored Teaching is adjustment of instructor input according to need. The instructor must know which material does need which methods for which students. Not everyone needs a lecture on everything, and some need more than mere lecture on important stuff. From experience with past students, I will sort content for application of various teaching methods, but you must participate in sorting. You must read the assigned readings on time, and you must identify which content areas you want the most extra help with. Tailored Teaching means each individual and each group and the whole class get what is needed from the instructor and from other sources.

Writing-to-Learn is the use of self-communication and multiple drafts to develop one's own understanding. Key features of writing to learn are that one must think to write and one must read one's own written words and re-think what was written about. Writing is how scholars develop their ideas and how anyone can come to know and measure one's own understanding. Our course will include bribes to develop the habit of frequent writing of multiple drafts. Some writing will be for self-feedback, but some will be read to peers or by the instructor. By doing lots of writing we will be doing lots of thinking, and we will learn to communicate more clearly and effectively. Writing by hand and by word processor will be practiced, and, while grammar, spelling, and neatness of handwriting are less important than thinking, presentable writing reveals that one can communicate and cares to do so.

Collaborative Learning is the third feature of ALFF; it relies on students helping each other learn. The help comes primarily in providing feedback as students let each other hear and react to early attempts at learning. Collaboration is how businesses succeed and how scholars develop ideas; it is a process which takes time and is work. Collaboration requires the communication skills to make one's ideas clearly understood and to offer clear reactions to peers.

This professor is committed to active participative student learning experiences. Cooperative assignments are designed to develop and demonstrate critical thinking and persuasive skills in ways individual assignments cannot. Cooperative groups are employed for three reasons: a) Tasks can be accomplished with greater success and less burden when shared, b) Teamwork, interpersonal persuasion, leadership and cooperation are essential career success determinants; they are best learned in practice, while consequences for difficulties are limited, c) Individuals help each other learn in more different and tailored ways than any one text or one lecture can accomplish.

Groups can be frustrating, especially to good students who lose feelings of control over their own success. Groups do take longer than working individually. I would not require group work if it were not more effective. Education research confirms that collaborative learning is so effective, partly because it provides immediate feedback in team reactions and calls for higher levels of support for choices in convincing teammates.

Some students will be more frustrated than others. Some will find extreme difficulties working with either teammates selected for them or ones they have chosen. See me to discuss frustrations and solution alternatives. I am not a therapist, but your frustrations are unlikely to be new ones and coping mechanisms of past students are easy to share.

It is better to learn collaboration at low cost now than to perhaps make costly errors early on in a professional career. I can not tell you how to cooperate, but I will help you adjust as you attempt and struggle at working together.

"DARING" TEACHING
Keshav Bhattarai, Eastern Kentucky University

Sometimes effective teaching involves stepping outside the box, perhaps even throwing the box away.

Teaching is one of my favorite jobs because of my culture and personal interest. I focus on Classroom Assessment Techniques (CATS) for effective teaching. I strongly believe that open forums for the exchange of ideas and materials are the essential ingredients of successful teaching. Very often, teaching becomes a thankless job, but I never shy away from open discussions of different theoretical issues. As Kuhnian philosophy says, ideas should be subjected to falsification and verification; we should not mind constructive criticisms.

There are various ways of teaching. Some people believe that asking questions and expecting every answer from students is the only innovative idea and all others are outdated pedagogical approaches and content delivery types, but I differ from this view. Methods of extracting every solution from students could be a good approach for upper-division classes where the student population is more or less homogeneous (in terms of academic standards), but for lower-division classes that are comprised of students from various disciplines and backgrounds, the approach of extracting every answer from the students might not work well, given the limitations of time and the students' attitude toward a particular subject. At first a teacher should stimulate the students' thinking and then involve students to moderate what has just been said. Students feel comfortable once they are exposed to a certain theme.

In a timely manner the instructor should provide/direct reading materials to students. In the class, a teacher should go through these reading materials to stimulate students' thinking. Once the students are energized, each student could work as a moderator of the subject the teacher has just presented. This step is very important in teaching universities. The majority of my students work full time and have very limited time to study. Very often the students' studies are limited only to the classroom. If we believe that asking questions to students at the very beginning is the only innovative approach to teaching, then we are degrading the quality of education because we are excessively relying upon students who might not have time to study before the class. However, if we first explain the concept and create an intuitive environment, then students could come up with new ideas.

I always follow the principle developed by the Teaching and Learning Center (TLC) here that taught me "*pairing* and sh*aring*," but I want to add one more word to this—"*daring*." Why I want to use this word is because we need to pair and share our ideas and then create a conducive environment to encourage students. This process is possible only when they are given a little clue of the subject matter at the beginning so that they can come up as moderators.

II. PRACTICES AND POLICIES

Equally as important to the overall success of a class as the approach we take are those practices and policies we establish to insure the class's smooth operation on a day-to-day basis. Certainly, we want to be fresh, to have spark of spontaneity that will make our classes alive and lively. On the other hand, we want to build our semesters on a strong foundation in order to get the most from each session.

This section presents some foundational elements that you can incorporate into your classes on a regular basis in order to supercharge those moments you spend with your students. The suggestions run the gamut from how to open a class to how to get things moving smoothly to how to bring a class to an effective close. As with the suggestions throughout this book, these tips are easily adaptable to most any discipline and can be used as presented or act as a springboard for your own creation.

PRE-COURSE CLASS PREPARATION

THE WEEKLY OVERVIEW
Hal Blythe and Charlie Sweet, Eastern Kentucky University

Effective teaching sometimes necessitates more than a five-day workweek.

Being in the right frame of mind to teach a class is obviously a good thing, but how do you get there? Just as we think it important to preview and review during each class period, so we believe it's helpful to preview and review each course on a weekly basis.

The first thing to do is bring a copy of each syllabus home. Each night we meticulously check off the class we taught that day: Jan. 14 Whitman. Then we make a brief note afterwards if there's anything we thought we should have covered or want to emphasize. The next time we go into class, that written note reminds us of something we need to bring up.

More importantly, each Sunday night we pick up the packet of syllabi and glance at the week ahead. We're mentally priming the pump, concentrating on how the individual units fit together, what we need to stress. Having the notes at home obviously in time and place alone gives us a different perspective on what we teach (mental preparation is especially important in lower-division courses we've taught so many times we think we could do it again in our sleep).

And that kind of reflection is always a good reflection on us.

FOLDERS
David J. Tarver, Angelo State University

A simple, but effective way of collecting your students' work.

As a first-year faculty member, I have been overwhelmed with all the preparation and grading required to be an effective teacher. Organization is paramount and I have limited access to a graduate assistant to help with the daily routines. I quickly figured out if I asked my students to turn in their tests, scantrons, assignments, etc. in an accordion folder (with pockets labeled A through Z) according to their last name, I'd save myself considerable time— time previously spent alphabetizing prior to recording grades and/or returning the graded materials. My students caught on very quickly and even began placing their material in alpha order within the individual letters.

These types of folders are available at nominal costs (compared to the amount of time I spent on alphabetizing prior to their purchase) at most office supply stores and come in sizes that accommodate 8 1/2 x 11 sheets as well as a size that is perfect for scantrons. I'm even saving instructional class time by returning materials in alpha order (my seating chart is alpha based).

MULTIPLE OUTSIDE SOURCES
Robert L. Burns

Everybody gets by better with a little help from friends.

When you are putting together your plans for next semester's classes, include a variety of sources to enrich the term. Your students will benefit from exposure to as much instructional technology as you can skillfully integrate into your presentations, so prepare to include video, interactive television, Internet, satellite broadcasts, and other technology that is available to you. But don't forget the human resources that are just down the hall or in the next building.

Guest lecturers from among your department colleagues or from related disciplines are always possible. Often untapped resources can be found among the administrative and support staff. The registrar who did her thesis on Hopkins or the director of Health Services whose dissertation featured aspects of the crises in Sudan might be eager to put together a class presentation that will enliven your course and bring new insights to your students.

Don't overlook the top executive officers, almost all of whom have the formal credentials to teach, but often lack the opportunity. You may find that the dean and the president are more than willing to have their classroom talents pulled down from the shelf for fifty minutes now and then. The experience will be educational for both students and the guest lecturers.

"WE WILL, WE WILL . . . ROCK YOU"
Hal Blythe and Charlie Sweet, Eastern Kentucky University

Music hath charms ...

The most important moment *of* class may not be *in* class. The solution to this riddle is found in class preparation, but not in doing the research, making notes, or even thinking about how you want to present the material.

Did you ever play a sport in school, or have you ever watched how professional athletes prepare for the upcoming contest, especially in those few moment just before a game? With today's generation of athletes, the favored method is music. But they don't just clamp earphones around their brain; they use their "tunes" to help them focus on the soon-to-begin competition.

We have adopted their methodology. We started with a cassette player that was eventually joined by a CD player. In the two or three minutes before class, we often drop in a tape or disk and rock out. In college Charlie had a teacher who defined music as magic, unsolicited response from a distance, and this magic is what music provides us in those precious last moments before class.

Why is music effective? Perhaps it drowns out all background sounds, and having no white noise makes it easier to concentrate. And, since most of the songs we choose are upbeat rock classics such as "We Are the Champions," "Walking in Memphis," "Pretty Woman," and "Stay," they recall a simpler time, remind us of fun, or help us to go with the positive flow. Try to be down after listening to Freddy Mercury claim "We will, we will . . . rock you." Try to worry about getting that set of tests graded while Chumbawawa's "I get knocked down, but I get up again" fills the office.

As we English teachers tell our class, "Ain't no mountain high enough to keep me from getting to you."

FIRST DAY

STUDENT INFORMATION
Merita Thompson, Eastern Kentucky University

Robert Frost once said it's impossible to hate someone up close . . .

On Day 1, I often hand out the following form to each student:

Name: Work Phone: Home Phone:
- Home Address:
- E-mail address:
- Major and Minor:
- Hobbies, interests, other things about yourself:
- What do you expect to get out of this class?
- What do you expect from me?
- What can I do to make learning easier or more comfortable for you?

On the back of this sheet, describe how you learn best. (For example, do you like to work alone or in groups? Do you like lecture, small group discussions, speakers, analysis of case stories, videos, class discussions with the instructor, etc.?)

E-MAIL INSTRUCTIONS
Kathy Mowers, Owensboro Community College

You've got mail . . .

My first assignment of the semester is to ask students to email me from their own account the answer to a question that doesn't require any particular expertise. Requests such as, "Email me your thoughts and feelings on problem solving or statistics," provide me insights into my students' backgrounds. Even more importantly, I can easily capture each student's email address.

WEB USE
Kathy Mowers, Owensboro Community College

Was it Spiderman who had the first website?

I am now keeping my students' grades on one of the course websites that is available for free to faculty members. My students report that they appreciate the more immediate feedback, and I have found that my errors are caught more quickly and easily than in years past.

PREVIOUS STUDENTS AS VISITORS
Judith E. Heady, University of Michigan-Dearborn

Who said you can't go home again?

On the first or second day of class in my Introductory Biology course, I have a student who has been in my courses previously come to talk with the class about the value of working in groups and to answer their questions. I leave the room so that the class can comfortably ask whatever they have in mind. My previous student is very positive, but was not that way in the beginning and she shares that too. This tactic has helped many wary students get over at least some of the doubts and fears.

MACARONI ART
Alice Jones, Eastern Kentucky University

An old proverb says sometimes the best icebreaker is a piece of macaroni.

In seminar-type classes, sometimes it's difficult to get students to shake the "sage on stage" mindset and to engage in active discussion. On the first day of a seminar-type class, I try to do some activity that is just totally unexpected. A favorite is macaroni art—really! Even with grad students!

I have a box full of dried macaroni and paper clips and buttons and string and bits of construction paper and Popsicle sticks and other silly craft-type stuff. I divide the class into groups of 3—4 students, then give each group the assignment to use this paraphernalia to illustrate some key term or concept related to the class. For example, in a public policy class, I might assign the groups the words "government," "power," "equity," "justice," and "community."

The usual reaction is that the students look at me suspiciously, then get into their groups and mumble to each other about how stupid it is to be a college senior doing kindergarten stuff. They laugh, they roll their eyes and shake their heads, and then they finally start fiddling around with the craft supplies. I give them about 15 minutes to create their masterpieces; then I allow each group to explain their work (or sometimes have the students try to guess what word each group was trying to express).

The most important part of the exercise is the debriefing. I ask students why in the world I have seniors and grad students doing macaroni art. Among the things they discover are:

1) The activity forms cohesion among class members—rolling their eyes and sharing a laugh at their nutty professor's expense becomes a little bonding experience that then helps the individuals begin developing a true learning community and working together as a group.

2) They overcome the shyness or embarrassment of speaking out in class. After you've played with Popsicle sticks in front of each other, how can sharing an opinion later in the semester possibly make you feel any sillier?

3) It highlights alternate forms of communication and makes more verbal students recognize that their quieter peers also have important contributions to make to the class. Less verbal students—including deaf students, international students who are self-conscious about their English, and those who are just shy—often become their group's leader in this activity because they are more comfortable expressing themselves in this visual medium.

4) Finally (and perhaps most importantly), they agree that sometimes our expectations limit our ability to consider all of the possibilities in a given situation.

FAMILY TREE
Sue Reimondo, Eastern Kentucky University

Getting back to your roots is a great way to get to know others.

In addition to asking students to introduce themselves on the first day of class, I ask each student to tell us where his/her name came from—why they were given the name they were given. This expression is especially suitable for first year orientation classes and classes with a focus on multicultural themes. I preface the exercise with an explanation that it is important to understand where we come from to fully appreciate the journey of an education. Students often express an appreciation for their heritage and their family lineage (since many are named after grandparents, etc.). Many students become more curious about their ethnic and cultural origins and begin to satisfy that curiosity by asking questions of different family members. As you can see, this method is a great way to introduce a research project! An added bonus is that this exercise has worked amazingly well in helping students (and myself) learn each others' names.

WASTE NOT, WANT NOT
Robert L. Burns

But one chance to make a first impression.

Don't surrender even a minute of your first class meeting. There is too much to do.

You will want to make the "class plan" clear. Students will appreciate hearing how you see this particular class relating to those they took last semester or will take next year. You will need time for housekeeping chores relating to attendance policy, class participation, and a lot more. And one of the most important things you can achieve that first hour is to begin to establish yourself as a personal link for your students.

Whether they are wide-eyed freshmen or savvy seniors, students will be more successful (and will stay in school longer) when they see you as a source of help and support. Take a few minutes to let your students know that you understand the issues and challenges they are facing outside your classroom. This admission is an important facet of the communication you and they will need for a successful educational experience.

Don't make the mistake of trying to be teacher, counselor, financial aid technician, campus nurse, and dorm mother all rolled into one. Your primary job is to teach. But you can be an important support element to your students if they see you as ready to listen and to refer them to the right places to find solutions to their many issues. That means you will have to maintain a basic awareness of those institutional resources, of course, so that you know where help can be found. Keep in mind that the quicker a student forms those helpful links to you and others at the institution, the more successful the student will be. Isn't that our goal?

TESTING AND QUIZZING

THE TEST
Bruce Davis, Eastern Kentucky University

To think, perchance to pass the test.

I often wonder about the real nature of tests and what they are supposed to examine. Although the study phase (preparation) is highly valuable, I have a difficult time accepting that a high pressure in-class think-fast, write-fast process has any real insight to a person's ability to use the information in the real world. Although there are numerous useful tricks to make those exams more appropriate and fair, I prefer to post the quizzes on the course web page, and give 3-4 days (preferably the weekend) to think and write up in-depth answers (as opposed to quickie responses in the in-class exams). My expectations can be elevated to demand demonstration of real knowledge and more professional presentation. This method works and students prefer the format. It's the most fair way I've given tests in over 20 years of teaching (although I'm not thoroughly convinced tests are really pertinent).

QUIZZES
Bruce Davis, Eastern Kentucky University

A written excuse. . .not from your mom.

Of course, I am an authority for the class material, but I also understand that I cannot think of every possible valid answer for questions and cannot always second guess valid alternative thinking. Therefore, I permit a defense of lost points on quizzes and assignments. Rather than haggling over points in person at the end of class, I ask that a one-paragraph defense be submitted by the next meeting. It must be a legitimately justifiable response, not something like "Well, I thought the answer was B instead of A." It must be well considered and neatly presented. I try to give benefit of doubt and use rather liberal interpretations of the questions. About 75% of the submissions get part or full credit in return, not because I am nice but for those who have carefully considered their answers, there is some demonstrated validity, e.g., some proof of their alternate perception. This practice saves much argument and is a fair evaluation strategy. It has worked for several decades.

BONUS ROUND
Hal Blythe and Charlie Sweet, Eastern Kentucky University

Extra credit with a value-added bonus

We've found that one of the most effective techniques for assuring that students read our assignments and come to class ready to discuss them is the daily reading quiz. To open each class, we give five questions on the assignment. These questions call for answers of a phrase or less and cover only surface concerns (e.g., "How old is the story's protagonist?" or "Who wins the race at the story's end?"). These quizzes not only get students to class on time (Questions aren't repeated for late arrivers), but also foster confidence in students by providing a positive start to the session.

Sometimes, however, even those students who diligently read the material stumble on a question or two from a long assignment. To combat this problem, we have developed a bonus question, a sixth question that can be substituted for one of the first five. This bonus question serves an additional purpose since we always pull it from the previous session's notes rather than the reading assignment. As a result, students have added incentive to review their notes from the previous class, something we all wish our students would do regularly.

The technique is a winner for both the students and us.

INDIVIDUAL QUIZZES
Wallace R. Wood, University of Cincinnati

Another Pardoner's Tale.

Here's another handout I provide my accounting students on opening day:
Individual Quizzes will be reading-based essays from the end-of-the-assignment questions. If you have read the assignment, the quiz will be your reward for being there and being prepared. I will score on content and writing performance as will be done on CPA Type Exams (and in most business situations), but I'm a lot more forgiving on live in-class writing than homework. You

must write in prose, using grammar and complete sentences, and of course legibility is the minimum requirement.

Just before an individual quiz, groups of students will be asked to identify the one **Barabbas** question they do not want to be asked. The pardoned question will later be answered for that group in writing or for the whole class as a **Request Lecture**. The purpose of this exercise is to discuss the possible questions before the quiz and to help sort reading into that content learned well by just reading it from content which requires Professor explanation to a small group or to the whole class.

In parallel with frequent feedback to students on homework and quizzes, the students will be required to provide feedback to the teacher on **Minute Papers,** which will be rewarded as individual quizzes. The minute paper helps the Professor know what you think was learned and what you don't think was learned. It is the first thing read after class and the guide as to what to do in the next class session.

QUIZ BARGAINING
Hal Blythe and Charlie Sweet, Eastern Kentucky University

When can not giving a quiz be more effective than giving one?

Did you ever have a day when you have a quiz all made up for class, but just don't feel like giving it? Of course you have, and sometimes it's for the simple reason you may not feel like it/have time to grade it. Don't just give up on the quiz, though; instead, use it in class as leverage.

Quizzes often become the Damoclean swords of a class. Students realize quite early that if they don't read the material, they are going to fail the quiz, and quizzes make up a good proportion of the final course grade (yes, we advocate daily quizzes in almost every class in almost every period, but you read that earlier). As a result, teachers often feel trapped; they hate not to give a quiz because that might send a wrong message to the class that quizzes will no longer be forthcoming on a regular basis.

Here is an alternative. Use the quiz as a bargaining chip. The pattern is quite simple. All you say is something to the effect of, "If I don't give you a quiz, what do you promise in return?" The possibilities are as boundless as your imagination.

In Charlie's World Lit II, for instance, he starts his second class with a quiz on Pope's "Essay on Man," a selection that makes giving an easy quiz an impossibility. Now this quiz is also the class's first (with day one being an introduction to the material), and Charlie doesn't want them to think they will get out of quizzes every day. Here's what he does. After five questions that would seemingly stump even presidents of MENSA, he holds up the collected quizzes over a wastebasket and tells them he will drop the quizzes in if they can do one thing: "Convince me to trash them, but you must do so in the manner of a good Neoclassic arguer." Gradually the students figure out they must appeal to Charlie's reason, not his emotions (a la "Because you're a nice guy"). One student once even came up with a Neoclassic heroic couplet: "The quizzes should become trash/Because I did what you asked." That statement generated a couple of "You go, girls" as well as a good discussion. Would, Charlie asked, a good Neoclassic use the first person? Hal has used the threat of a quiz to extract all sorts of promises ranging from "Honest, we'll discuss the material, Dr. Blythe" to "Can we write up some alternate questions for you?"

In *Pee-Wee's Big Adventure*, Francis makes the statement that his dad says all things are negotiable. Even quizzes, Francis.

GROUP TESTING
Ken Clawson, Eastern Kentucky University

A lifeline in the classroom

Another application of cooperative learning groups comes as I allow my students to work together on my multiple choice objective part of tests. They must discuss each question; then each marks his/her own answer. Usually they reach concensus. This process does two things: it reduces the stress of testing, and it continues the learning at a point of prior study and a high motivation period. (I always have students also writing on short answer, discussion questions on each test, and they must do this on their own.)

Cooperative learning groups foster a bonding and team spirit among students as the semester progresses. They may call one another or share information outside the classroom when needed.

COLLABORATIVE CREATIVE QUIZZES
Tammy Horn, Eastern Kentucky University

If two heads are better than one, what about three. . .or four?

I like my students to apply the principles of the authors we are discussing in a creative manner, but didn't realize how much fun they would have doing it. The idea is this: after students have learned a variety of genres, instead of giving them an ordinary quiz, I ask them to break into groups, and then I give each group a different genre to create. For example, in my world literature class, I asked one group to write a myth about a successful football coach; another group to write a hymn to our president; another group to create a fable for freshman; and a final group to create a psalm to the governor. These collaborative quizzes are successful because students are guaranteed ten points as long as the group has incorporated the appropriate characteristics of the genre they are asked to create (for example, an animal has to be in a fable). In addition, the anxiety students often experience with objective quizzes is eliminated for one quiz. More importantly, this type of quiz rewards a student's active application of material learned during lectures and creativity. For what it's worth, I generally plan this type of quiz after two traditional quizzes so those students who haven't done well on the traditional quiz format can bring that portion of their grade up

THE QUOTE SELECTION PROCESS
Tammy Horn, Eastern Kentucky University

To be, or not to be. . .included—that is the question.

One of the consistent criticisms that students had of my literature exams was the quote identification section in which they were asked to identify important quotes, the texts in which they appeared, and explain their importance to the overall context of the work. At best, the majority of students were convinced I picked quotes we had never discussed in class, and I suspect that most thought I made quotes up in the middle of the night.

Now, the day before the test, I decide which tools I want to emphasize (i.e., character, setting, structure, etc.). I put those three tools on the board. Then, I ask the students to go through the readings picking out one quote from all the readings which best exemplifies each tool. Students should have three in about ten minutes.

Then, I ask my students to form groups. They select the best choices of those quotes that the students bring to the group. I generally insist that the quote be clearly identified with a tool and that it reflects a characteristic of a time period, such as Modernism. Each group writes its three choices on a sheet of paper. Each sheet is then brought to the front of the classroom. And, depending upon how much time I have left, I pick quotes at random and discuss how a tool is working effectively in the quote and its importance to the story and/or poem overall. I always make the "student pool" available to the students at the end of class and in my office.

I have been asked if this process is "teaching the test." My response is that I teach them how to take the test by directing their attention back to the text. Ironically, I have had groups that chose quotes that I considered too difficult to put on the test. My class had a good time seeing why I wouldn't put some quotes on the test because they didn't have any identifying features or clues. All in all, this process makes the quote identification section seem less arbitrary than what it had been before.

POSTING TEST ANSWERS
Richard Stanislaw, Waynesburg College

Tell it like it is. . .after the exam.

Here's a really simple habit that captures the teachable moment:
Whenever I give an exam that has "right and wrong" answers (such as identifying a composer or event), I post the answers on the outside of the door to the room so the students can look at them after they have turned in the exam but before they have stopped caring about it.

SELF-POSED POST-TEST QUESTIONS
Rose Pennington, Eastern Kentucky University

Well, at least they knew something.

Sometimes when students are preparing for an exam, something that they felt was very valuable (and for which they studied and were very prepared to be tested on) is not included on an exam I give. I encourage students to report this omission on the bottom of the exam and they will be given some credit.

MAKEUPS
Wallace R. Wood, University of Cincinnati

Remember when you messed up a play on the schoolyard and pleaded for a "do over"?

Here's a system I've found effective for handling makeup work. I provide students in all my classes with the following statement:

Early, late, or substitute homework and/or quizzes are not acceptable. For most homework, bringing it to class with you is the only way to fully participate in class, and sending your work early or late would not replace that in-class use of the assignment. It is very hard to create a replacement assignment that is fair to other class members, and it is difficult enough to keep up without working double time to get ahead or to catch back up.

If you miss any assignment, type up a "borderline letter" to be read at quarter grade assignment time **only if you are on the edge** between two term grades. The letter should describe the **score you would have received** and include any pitiful reasons life interfered with your receiving that score. With the plus-minus grades, many students are near a term grade borderline, but even a stack of borderline letters won't move you across multiple grades.

INDIVIDUAL AND TEAM HOMEWORK AND QUIZZES
Wallace R. Wood, University of Cincinnati

Some teachers prefer a complete system for handling quizzes and homework.

To make the process of quizzes and homework both clear and consistent, I include the following in my syllabus:

Individual Homework will be a one typed page essay on topics assigned the week before. Essays must have names only on the back so the grader can read and sort the paper before knowing who wrote it. Do not cheat me of my opportunity to be fair. Names are also on the back to allow some privacy in returning papers. It should be possible to find and pick out one's own work without looking at comments or scores on anyone else's papers. Please be polite and remember there are lots of assignments, so peeking at anyone's paper should be no cause for sympathy or glee.

Homework is typed because then it is exactly clear what was done BEFORE arriving in class and what was added during class discussion, which almost always precedes collecting papers. Typed papers are also easier to read and easier to read without guessing the author from handwriting.

Individual essays should encourage every student to be creative and analytical in thought. They should provide feedback on comprehending instructions on expressing ideas in writing and will force thinking. These are assignments to develop more than memory.

Individual Essays will be sorted by content and by writing clarity. Do your best to make your thoughts clear with standard grammar and spelling. Whenever possible, use paragraphs and sentences to separate and emphasize the outline of your different ideas, examples and reasons.

Ethics essays will be sorted by reasoning, evidence, and expression. If you agree with me completely but do not explain why, you will get low scores. If you do not write/spell like a professional, I will score your paper as if you do not care. Continue to ignore conventions of our language, and professionals will score your work as if you do not know better.

Part of each assignment is to develop your self-awareness. By explaining why you hold your opinions, you will come to know yourself and will prepare to more quickly understand other people. It is fine to be different in beliefs, but not acceptable to be unable to understand or express differences.

These assignments are often chances to be original and creative and demonstrate that you quickly and clearly understand directions. Do make sure you do understand directions and that your paper says what you mean to say. Discuss it with your classmates or other colleagues, but of course write your own paper.

Individual Quizzes will be reading-based essays from the end of chapter questions. If you have read the chapter, the quiz will be your reward for being there and being prepared I will score on content and writing ability, but I'm a lot more forgiving on live in-class writing than homework. Often Writing-to-Learn will be done just for feedback, without points assigned.

Team Homework will be problems assigned the week before. Team members participating will receive equal credit. Team homework is to be done together so that team members help each other learn. Playing spin the bottle or taking turns is forbidden and stupid. Team problems are assigned to teams specifically because group discussion and shared solution are an essential part of the learning experience.

Team Quizzes will consist of objective questions such as fill-in-the-blank or matching and are open-book/open-note but one answer for the team. Persuade each other using logic and evidence. Team quizzes are exercises in persuasion and opportunities to help each other learn and to individually assess progress. Failing to participate cheats the team members and especially the absent individual. Team members should not persuade each other on bases of authority, power, or even voting. These problems are made valuable specifically by the debate required to achieve consensus.

Team Homework and Quizzes are usually scored as 5, 6, 7, 8 or 9 points…or 0 if missing. The number of total points possible varies from term to term.

WRITE YOUR OWN FINAL
Wallace R. Wood, University of Cincinnati

Granting the student's ultimate wish.

"Write-Your-Own-Final" procedures provide a quality comprehensive exam, comparable to instructor sorted test bank exams, but also provide an activity that encourages students and provides them confidence and satisfaction with comprehensive exams. Students write questions they want to be asked as they learn, and those questions are used for weekly diagnostic quizzes and then stored and sorted for test assembly. Students often record, trade, and assemble a comprehensive bank of all their submitted questions, which are then used to study in a quizzing active way. Some students will memorize the entire bank—which should cover what they need to remember out of the course.

The technique was invented to help students recognize what content they are learning and to recognize questioning at the various levels of Bloom's taxonomy. "Write-Your-Own-Final" teaches students to dissect and understand multiple choice in ways only question writers are likely to do well. It also passes responsibility for what is fair coverage to students and allows learning responsibility to develop in areas not "covered" in classroom lectures. Students consistently rate "Write-Your-Own-Final" as the most popular of Active Learning Frequent Feedback strategies.

Write-Your-Own-Final Rules:
1. Write questions **as you learn**, right after reading, right after class lecture or discussion, and right after team work on homework cases or project.
2. Write questions with stems that would allow you to "**look for**" the ending that completes the sentence or answers the question.

3. **Avoid negative** forms such as, "Which of these is not true?" or "Which is not a member of this list?"
4. Write questions on a **4x6 index card**—no other medium will do.
5. Write **legibly**—if typist has to struggle reading, the question is dropped rather than inflicted on class with wrong word or spelling.
6. Use **four or five answers** and make them relatively **short** compared to the Question Stem.
7. If "**All of these**" is a possible answer, it must be **first** among your answers.
8. If "**None of these**" is a possible answer, it must be **last** among your answers.
9. Attempt to make **wrong answers** that sound **plausible** but are clearly **not correct**.
10. Avoid **word for word** extraction from text questions—they are gender biased.
11. Questions must have **"correct"** answer **identified**. If the instructor and question writer disagree about which answer is best, the question will be dropped AND the topic reviewed in class or individually.
12. The instructor may **add** questions **to balance** coverage across course topics and question types.
13. **Write** questions of **various types**: definitions, problems, and application of concepts as well as techniques.
14. Write **at least one question per week** but preferably one per day. The more good ones you write, the better your chances of seeing your own question on the final exam.
15. **Keep a copy of questions** you submit and study by quizzing each other in groups.
16. Some questions will be read aloud at the beginning of class and these should serve as **editing** and writing advice and as a **secret quiz** for you to check yourself on how you would do on a final exam to date.

CLASS ORGANIZATION

PREVIEWING
Steve Fardo, Eastern Kentucky University

Sometimes the best part of movie going wasn't the popcorn but the previews.

Effective communication between the instructor and the student is essential. An important way to improve communication is to plan effective introductions. The **introduction** sets the stage for a lesson. An old adage is to "tell them what you are going to tell them, tell them, and then tell them what you have told them." This phrase reminds us that it is important to use reinforcement, beginning and ending reviews, and effective communication techniques during the instructional process.

ALL GOOD THINGS MUST END—EFFECTIVELY
Hal Blythe and Charlie Sweet, Eastern Kentucky University

It's not over till...

In over a dozen years of mentoring teachers, we've found the single biggest problem with class comes at the end. Teachers have trouble pulling things together effectively. More often than not, the session ends with the teacher yelling an assignment at students as they race from the room or simply stopping *in medias sentence* when the clock strikes end of period.

For us, the last few minutes of class can be the most important, for it is during this time that you can pull things together from the entire hour, insure that students take away the class's most important points, and set up the next class meeting.

The session's last five minutes or so provide a great opportunity for you to pull together the material you've presented by way of review. You might choose to touch on the class's major points by rewriting them on the board or calling them up again via power point. You might additionally provide a context for the session by showing students how the day's material fits into the semester's larger scheme. Students always want to know specific material's place in the "big picture."

The last few minutes can also be used to make sure students have understood the session's material. You might choose simply to ask a few pointed questions, or you might opt to have students write out what they believe were the class's most important points. You might even decide on a quick end-of-class quiz over the covered material. A colleague of ours often asks students to write out one question they have about the day's material. The key is variety.

You can also use the last segment of class to set up the next session. Forecast what you'll be doing and how the current day's material prepares students for that session. This type forecast brings even more continuity to the semester, allowing students to feel confident about where they are, where they're going, and how they'll get there.

Make your class end not with a whimper but with a bang, a big bang.

PRESENTATION TECHNIQUES

DEMONSTRATIONS
Steve Fardo, Eastern Kentucky University

Not all demonstrations appear on the 2:00 a.m. infomercials.

The demonstration method of teaching is considered the best way to teach certain skills. Demonstrations consist of displaying equipment, tools or materials to show correct procedures or processes. Cognitive skills may also be taught by the demonstration method. When an instructor discusses a process step-by-step, teaching can be very effective. The visual element involved in demonstrations adds to the student's long-term learning. The instructor can stop at any time during a demonstration to check understanding and provide students an opportunity to ask questions. Demonstrations are not just for scientific and technical disciplines. Almost any subject area could utilize demonstrations to facilitate learning.

Videotaping can also be done in conjunction with demonstrations. For example, a process could be shown step-by-step with repeated viewing opportunities for students. Demonstrations require careful planning and practice before being conducted. They can be used to emphasize the instructor's skill and knowledge and to provide a model or standard for what is expected of students.

POWER POINT
Larry C. Bobbert, Eastern Kentucky University

Be a Power-Arranger.

Teachers who create Power Point and other "show 'n tell" presentations need to remember "a picture is worth a thousand words."

PROPS
Julie George and Kari Lyons, Eastern Kentucky University

You gotta give your class their "props."

The monotony of sitting in classes hour after hour and day after day can often take its toll on both students and teachers. The repeated process of lectures and note taking often serves only to enhance students' boredom in the classroom instead of sparking curiosity in their capable minds.

In an effort to jazz up note taking and add a creative touch to course content, we created a special collection of props and tools useful for classroom instruction. Each item in the collection is designed to encourage creativity in teaching as well as encourage student participation and interactive learning. The collection contains items such as scented markers, colored paper, candy, index cards, a Koosh ball, post-its, and a deck of cards. These items along with numerous others add a special twist to classes in many fields of study. While such items may seem small and insignificant, they can serve as quick, inexpensive, creative, and interesting ways to spice up potentially dry class sessions.

The use of these teaching materials forces the instructor to think beyond normal classroom activities and strive for ways to be creative and unique both in presentation and instruction. Taking part or all of the collection to class allows the instructor to quickly add a creative touch to the class content. Likewise, having parts of the collection in the classroom reminds one to remain flexible, creative, and willing to run where the students' discussions and inquiries lead. With the right tools, props, and preparedness, the monotony of traditional lectures is destroyed by the creativity of non-traditional presentation.

CONCERNS

BLOCK OF CHEESE DAY
Hal Blythe and Charlie Sweet, Eastern Kentucky University

Say Cheese . . . once a semester.

Sometimes we borrow teaching techniques from our colleagues, occasionally we run into a good idea while doing research, and often we discover new approaches at our Teaching & Learning Center. But as teachers who employ more pop culture references each class than Buffy does per episode, we admit we adapted this idea from network television.

In Aaron Sorkin's fictional world, President Jeb Bartlett has executively ordered that one day each year *The West Wing* must hold Block of Cheese Day. The purpose of the event, inspired by a past president's opening the White House and serving cheese (Jackson, perhaps), is that groups that don't usually have access to the West Wing be given an opportunity.

In the real universe of our classroom, we hold Block of Cheese Day some time past mid-semester. Its purpose is to allow students to present ideas and to ask questions we might not ordinarily have time for. After all, with mandated detailed syllabi, the instructor's trying out various teaching techniques, and voluminous reading assignments, students are rarely allowed to wander off on tangents. Yet we have found that each student has something s/he has often wondered about the teacher, about the material, or about the basic worth of the class. Block of Cheese Day allows students to get these things off their chests.

Some of the questions we can anticipate. In our creative writing classes, students are dying to ask, "How do two guys write together as one?" or "Where do you guys get your ideas?" In lit classes someone always wants to know "Did the writer consciously put that element in?" or "What makes your interpretation better than mine?" Some questions come out of left field. "What was the English Romantics' favorite drug of choice?" and "Do you have to have a mental breakdown in order to become a famous poet?" Some queries are unanswerable and some are quite personal. Others are just fun, such as our creative writing class during a session on poetry asking us for our favorite pop lyrics of all time. Best rock rhyme? Greatest group?

Block of Cheese Day does a lot of things. Obviously it provides variety and it allows students to voice things that trouble them, especially matters that seem too trivial to ask. More than these, however, BOCD creates an open class-room atmosphere and contributes to a real rapport between teacher and student.

CHILDREN IN THE CLASSROOM
Hal Blythe and Charlie Sweet, Eastern Kentucky University

Mom always said there's a place for everything, just not in the classroom.

During our tenure as teachers we've seen an evolution in the type of student. Gone are the days of the single student approximately 18-22 years of age completing college in four years. Now our classes are laden with non-traditional students, married students, and older students, many of whom take up to six years to obtain their degree. And as the student population changes, so class policies have to be adjusted to accommodate these shifts.

One recent phenomenon is single parents, and so day-care is a problem. A worse problem occurs for us when school-age kids have a holiday or get snowed out because then their parents are apt to bring the kids to class. One May Intersession after public schools had let out, we had a single mom show up so often with her eight and nine-year-old boys that during some classes we had to compete with two kids using the hallway as a Hot Wheels track. Other times we've had students bring kids to class and sit them down with books, drinks, and crayons, the latter two often spilling during the class. We are not talking about simple distractions because even when kids are well behaved, students in class watch them, perhaps wondering when something will go wrong. And then there's the question of appropriateness. How does an instructor discuss D. H. Lawrence's sexual insights in "Odor of Chrysanthemums" or the violence of Margot Macomber's exploding her husband's skull with a bullet from a Mannlicher with a fourth-grader in the second row?

As a result of these experiences and other similar ones, we've adapted a no children in the classroom policy that shows up on the information sheet. Maybe grandmother was right and children should be seen and not heard, but we'd rather both actions were not options. In an emergency snow-day last semester, Charlie walked into his Am Lit class and saw a four-year-old crayoner ready to help discuss the Salem witch trials. He simply allowed the mother to take the daily quiz and had her arrange to have another student take the notes for her.

Yes, the parent has rights, but so do the paying students, and a child is not a paying student.

RESEARCH
Janet Klaessig, Delaware Valley College

The early bird gets the paper that hasn't been plagiarized.

Traditionally, we have been faced with two major problems concerning student term papers: papers based on inappropriate sources and the submission of plagiarized papers. Unfortunately, the exponential expansion in Internet sources has produced little improvement in the first problem and probably exacerbated the latter. Over the last two years we have devoted one lab period of an undergraduate science course, Animal Behavior, to the proper use of library resources, both print and online, with particular attention to electronic database subscriptions. Students are required to select their topics during this two hour session and to gather the appropriate literature in consultation with the instructor and a reference librarian present during the lab. This structure requires the student to produce a feasible topic supported by appropriate scholarly articles from databases demonstrated by the librarian during the lab. Special emphasis is given to the concept of peer-reviewed literature, its structure and its appearance in both paper and electronic formats. The librarian describes and assists students in using advanced search techniques to retrieve the most appropriate articles. The early submission of topics and references virtually eliminates both the use of poor reference material and the submission of plagiarized term papers.

YOUR MISSION: NOT IMPOSSIBLE
Hal Blythe and Charlie Sweet, Eastern Kentucky University

"Generally speaking"... is not a phrase you want to use in the classroom—especially when giving assignments

More often than not, teachers list reading assignments on their syllabi or give the assignment to the class orally in those last few hectic moments before (or after) the bell without the slightest guidance toward making the readings meaningful. And so often students come to the next class not having completed the reading ("I couldn't get into it" or "I got lost halfway through it") or with little understanding of the material.

We've come up with a strategy that both helps students understand their readings and acts as a springboard for discussion at the next section. Borrowing from an old television favorite, we create a "dossier" for each of our assignments, and before sending our students on their mission, we review the dossier (We haven't self-destructed in nearly 30 years of teaching) to provide them with the necessary information/ tools to complete the assignment successfully.

For our World Lit. students, poetry always represents a difficult (They think impossible) mission. When we assign Tennyson's "Ulysses," for instance, we see looks of desperation and hear the inevitable murmurs—"Oh, no, a Victorian writing a poem about a Greek renamed by the Romans." To allay these fears, we give them a list of *specific* things to look for as they read: Who is speaking in the poem? To whom is this person speaking? What is the person's social position? Where does the conversation take place? What is the subject of the conversation? Note that we don't ask, "What does the poem mean?" or some other general, intimidating question. The purpose of our "dossier" is simply to allow the students an entré to the poem, a way of comfortably confronting the material.

When the students arrive for the next class, we have a set of concrete questions whose answers provide easy victories for the class while at the same time building a solid foundation for our discussion of the dramatic monologue and its theme of Victorian optimism and never-give-in tenacity.

The dossier strategy is certainly not limited to literature. You could prepare Geography students for a tough article filled with research by foregrounding the assignment with information about the researcher and / or concrete questions, such as "What is the central issue that led to the research?" or "What is the researcher's thesis; how does he / she support it?" An assignment in Biology might be set up by giving students a problem then asking, "Can you find three major steps in solving the problem?"

GRADING
Cecilia Shore, Miami University (Ohio)

As on a ship, sometimes a small course correction means getting to your destination.

I use a grading system that I have found quite effective and students seem to like. On each exam, the best two scores will be averaged. This average will be the top of the curve for that exam (provided that this average is at least 95% of the original points possible). For example, if there were 50 questions possible on an exam and the best two scores were 48 and 49, their average is 48.5 (97% of the original total), so 48.5 will be the top of the curve. If there were 50 questions possible and the best two scores were 45 and 46, their average is less than 47.5 (95% of the original), so 47.5 would serve as the top of the curve. Each student's score is recorded as a percentage of the top of the curve for that exam. Because the top of the curve is determined by the best performance of the students' peers, there will be no items thrown out from the exam. If an item is bad, it will be missed by the best students and consequently not counted against any student. This approach saves incredible amounts of point-picking. Every student almost always gets to throw out a couple of questions, whichever ones were their least-favorites, and not argue with me about whether this was a "bad question" or not. The 95% rule means that I can still hold up my standards and expectations about what they should know, and yet be flexible in response to class performance. Over several years, I have compared the results of this method with other forms of item analysis (which questions did the top third of the class miss, which questions did everybody pile up on the same wrong answer, which questions did over half of the class miss, etc.) and find that this method generally works out to drop the same number of questions.

ASSESSMENT

THE END OF CLASS PARAGRAPH
Sonny Butler, Eastern Kentucky University

One more thing before we leave. . .

A technique I have started to use in my graduate class and intend to try in my undergraduate classes is about 5 minutes before the end of class I have each student write one paragraph on the lesson(s) learned for today. I call this your "take away" for today. My goal is for the student to take away the primary focus of the day's class. This technique makes them listen more carefully and maybe even make a note or two.

PERIODIC ASSESSMENT
John Jeep, Miami University (Ohio)

Why wait till the end?

My most effective assessment tool is the following:
- Start with a blank piece of paper.
- On the front: What aspects of this course are most productive for your learning?
- Back of sheet: How might the course be improved to meet your learning needs?
- Send it (multiple copies, if necessary) around the classroom.
- Make it clear that no one need sign the sheet(s).

The feedback lets me know what is working, and I often receive great ideas for improvement. I discuss the results briefly at the beginning of the next class and let students know how I hope to implement any adjustments, even if that means doing more of what works best.

END OF CLASS QUESTIONS
Keshav Bhattarai, Eastern Kentucky University

An assessment a day brings students your way.

I follow EKU's Teaching and Learning Center model of collecting feedback from each student at the end of each class. I believe that such a practice allows the teacher to review students' comments and quickly improve teaching in successive classes. Although people might disagree with this approach, my students are improving their grades. I use the following questions at the end of each class and review them carefully for each student's comments. My teaching has been greatly improved with this approach—"this works for me."
1. Are the notes clear and illustrative with examples?
2. What did you learn today?
3. Is the instructor clear in the discussed subject matter? Did he clearly communicate with you?
4. Does the instructor use examples that insult students' cultures?
5. How does the instructor treat you?
6. How could the instructor improve this class?

7. Is the course organization good?
8. Does the instructor address important issues that are listed in the course syllabus?
9. Would you like to suggest new ideas for the open book examination?
10. Do you have any suggestions to make this class much more effective than it is now?

Assurance: Your opinions will be kept confidential, and there is no penalty for being critical about the instructor and course. This is why I do not need your name written on this sheet.

SYLLABI AND INFORMATION SHEETS AS LEGAL DOCUMENTS
Hal Blythe and Charlie Sweet, Eastern Kentucky University

If you don't list your goals, you might go directly to . . .

One final word on syllabi and information sheets. Last semester we watched an episode of CBS-TV's *The Education of Max Bickford* wherein Chadwick's number-one professor got into a law suit. Max had deliberately lowered a student's grade on a paper each time she challenged the original grade and angered him. The president of this college (which seems to us set in Fantasy Land) read Max the riot act because he had not followed university policy as outlined in their guidebook.

Max, like a lot of professors, failed to realize we now live in a litigious age. Almost any dispute can/probably will be ultimately settled in a court of law. One area, though, that Max never considered and probably most instructors don't is the syllabus/information sheet that is usually handed out on the first day of class. Instructors ought to think of this document as a legal contract.

One thing we have done over the years is to split this document into a syllabus that details the daily assignments of the course and an information sheet that lists all of the applicable university and course-specific policies. We have tried to be as accurate as we can, updating the policies, spelling out examples, and clarifying the rules. Then we live by the document.

We have never had a grade challenged, but doubt we can go unscarred till retirement. Part of the reason, though, for our safety has been the thoroughness of our document and our continuing adherence to it. If you claim a quiz average will be 25% of the final grade, make sure you compute it that way. If you state that tardies will each be counted as one-half an absence, make sure you keep a detailed attendance record. If your school has a disability statement saying qualified students will be given extra time to finish tests, be certain you contact the proper authorities and offer your students this chance. If you promise to get all the tests back in the period after they are given, pull an all-night grading session so you fulfill your part of the bargain.

Experience has taught us some guidelines. If the school has a policy, list and follow it. Adjust the information sheet each semester if you know there are going to be special occasions where, for instance, you won't have time to grade papers immediately. Deal with student complaints immediately. If a student claims, "I was in class last time, Mrs. Jones," check to see if you have a record, be it even a quiz grade rather than an attendance mark. If you announce to your classes a policy and you screw up, correct your mistake. For instance, we each have a policy that if we didn't cover something in class/assign it on the syllabus, then it won't be on the test. Invariably we ask a question we neglected to go over or have them read, so in that case we give them full credit even though they might have missed a question. Keep your office hours. If you know you have a meeting called for that period, let your students know in advance as a courtesy. If you give your students your e-mail address, you have an obligation to write them back if they contact you.

With us, the information sheet and syllabus are even more than a potential court suit; they are a matter of respect. Dad always taught, "If you say you're going to do it, do it." That's self-respect and respect for others.

III. EXERCISES AND TECHNIQUES

While diversifying your approach to class and establishing certain foundational practices and policies will enhance your effectiveness, perhaps no single aspect of teaching impacts learning more than those individual, day-to-day exercises you offer your students. Exercises bring the material to life and call for students to confront the ideas and concepts you have presented in ways more concrete than demanded by general discussion. Whether the students deal with the exercise individually or in groups, they must demonstrate a sound understanding of underlying principles that far surpasses a nod of the head or a raised hand.

In this section you'll find a plethora of practical exercises designed to draw the most from students. As in other sections, you'll find some suggestions that seem inappropriate for your use, some that seem worth a try, and some that will spark you to create an exercise of your own that seems better fit. In any case, remember that these are exercises offered by teachers like you who work hard to make each class experience unique and valuable.

LITERATURE

THEIR "WRITE" TO UNDERSTAND

Hal Blythe and Charlie Sweet, Eastern Kentucky University

Guiding your students down the road not taken can be a valuable journey.

As teachers of both literature and creative writing, we have often encouraged our creative writing students to improve their writing skills by constantly reading the best literature available; imitation is more than simply the greatest form of flattery. In the last few years, however, we've realized that the relationship between literature and creative writing can be mutual beneficial. That is, we've learned that our literature students can gain much in terms of understanding the works they're studying by engaging in a few exercises in creative writing.

Have you ever read a work and felt confused or dissatisfied at the end? Gotcha! Well, this situation occurs often in our literature courses. Have you ever been tempted to "redo" that ending, to make it work better? That's exactly what we have our lit students do. Playing a creative writer's favorite game— "What if?"— we ask our students to create different endings for the works we're studying. For instance, what if Hedda Gabler hadn't shot herself at the end of the play; what would have happened the next evening at the Tesman house? What happened between Young Goodman Brown and his wife, Faith, the morning after their fateful meeting at the Black Mass? What did Ellison's unnamed protagonist tell his beloved Laura when he went home after losing the much-needed money at the bingo game?

Having our students rewrite endings enhances their understanding of the work in several ways. In order to create a new ending, they must work hard to fully grasp the nature of the characters and their relationships. Certainly, for example, students have to know Ellison's protagonist well before attempting to create a scene between him and his wife. Further, actually creating a fictional scene causes students to think more deeply about the author's style, use of setting, dialog. To become writers demands that these students immerse themselves in the work rather than simply reading it.

This creative technique can work outside the discipline of literature. What better way to understand Freudian psychology than to have students create a scene involving the good doctor and a patient? What about a scene in which Sir

Isaac Newton explains the aspect of physics? Or how about a scene involving an officer and a felon to make a principle of law come alive?

Regardless of your discipline, you can give your students deeper understanding by letting them exercise their "writes."

A PICTURE IS WORTH...
Hal Blythe and Charlie Sweet, Eastern Kentucky University

If seeing is believing, then students must be able first to picture what we want them to believe.

Psychologists tell us that more than three - quarters of what we learn enters through our eyes. This interesting statistic has led us to a novel, yet effective technique for helping our students understand literature: we have them create pictures that depict fictional characters and scenes.

Often with a work of literature students get lost in the avalanche of words, especially when reading prose from another age / culture or when confronting the quirky stylistics of poetry. Having them "picture" a character or scene makes the fiction come alive for them and helps them feel more comfortable in dealing with it. For instance, students get a better grasp of the plot of Ibsen's *Hedda Gabler* after drawing up a schematic (or even a picture) of the Tesman drawing room. This representation gives them a better understanding of where the play's entire action takes place, but also (when they add the small curtained room dominated by the huge portrait of Hedda's father behind the drawing room) they get a vivid insight into the struggle going on between Hedda's public and private personae. This realization allows them to understand Hedda's withdrawal at the play's end to the small room, away from the prying public, to commit suicide.

One of the most difficult works for American Lit students to "get into" is Jonathan Edwards' "Sinner's in the Hands of an Angry *God*"; to them, the classic Puritan sermon seems distant and filled with incomprehensible language. Their confusion is cleared up a bit, however, by having them picture a few of Edwards' colorful metaphors: we have them draw the sinners dangling over the fiery pit of hell on a single strand like spiders about to be committed to the blaze; our students create a picture of God holding the drawn bow about to loose a deadly arrow; and they even draw the consuming flood Edwards so forebodingly mentions. These images not only bring the sermon to life, but they help to show students the true brilliance of the Enfield Sermon—the images of destruction (fire, bow, flood) were all things the settlers feared not just on the spiritual level, but on the daily level as well as they combatted Indian raids and the flooding of nearby rivers.

Certainly, this graphic technique can be employed in disciplines other than literature. Having students picture historical events, pen cartoon versions of chemical reactions, create star charts for Astronomy, or depict accident scenes for Traffic Safety can effectively "draw" them into the materials.

ENGAGING STUDENTS THROUGH THE WRITINGS OF ARTHUR CONAN DOYLE
Ted Morrissey, Springfield College

It's Elementary...

Everybody loves a mystery. Or so it seems to me after teaching English for the past 19 years. Three years ago I introduced a mystery unit around the writings of Sir Arthur Conan Doyle, specifically his Sherlock Holmes tales. From a pedagogical standpoint, Conan Doyle's writing allows for a variety of critical thinking activities.

Beyond basic comprehension skills, the Sherlock Holmes stories lend themselves well to critical thinking opportunities. Because the tales are mysteries, students can analyze the clues as Holmes and Watson uncover them, and they can form their own theories about the case and its given suspects. While reading *The Hound of the Baskervilles* (one of the four novel-length stories), I have my students compile a list of suspects and clues; every three chapters they have to write a brief hypothesis about the case, incorporating the suspects and clues that have led them to this theory. As they read along, events of the novel either strengthen their theory or make it completely implausible, which forces them to formulate a new one.

Another activity related to *The Hound* that works well is a close reading of the text to create a sketch of the crime scene. In chapters two and three, Dr. Mortimer provides enough detailed information to Holmes and Watson about where Sir Charles Baskerville died that students—reading and thinking carefully—can sketch an accurate representation of the crime scene. Most students can relate to this type of activity because of all the cop shows they have seen on television, especially ones like "CSI" (Crime Scene Investigation) and "Profiler." From their reading, students gather the following details:

- Sir Charles's body was found at one end of the yew alley that connects Baskerville Hall to a summer-house; he was nearer the summer-house end but still fifty yards away from it.
- The footprints of a giant hound were found twenty yards from the body.
- The two rows of impenetrable yew hedge are twelve feet high; the path in the center is eight feet wide; there is a six foot strip of grass on either side of the path; on one side about half way along, a wicket gate leads to the moor; the hound footprints were on the edge of the path on the same side as the moor gate.
- The wicket gate, which is about four feet high, was closed and padlocked. Sir Charles must have stood at the gate for about ten minutes because there were two bits of cigar ash on the ground. From Baskerville Hall to the wicket gate, Sir Charles's footprints looked normal; from the gate to the point where his body was found, he seemed to be walking on his toes.

Using this information, a student should come up with a sketch.

The next logical step in the process is to re-create the crime scene. I have a fairly large classroom and I have used a seating arrangement for a number of years that is more or less theater-in-the-round with the student desks partially around the perimeter of the room and a large open space in the middle. This allows my students to create the *Baskerville* crime scene without disrupting the normal flow of the room. We have a student lie on the floor in the approximate position of the corpse; then another student outlines the body in masking tape. Students then use yard sticks to mark the eight-foot path and the six-foot strips of grass on either side, also in masking tape (by now we are into student-desk area—my room isn't that big). Students draw pictures of Baskerville Hall and the summer-house, and we tape these to opposite walls. We then tape pieces of paper to the floor with directional arrows, heights and distances to significant parts of the scene, like the wicket gate (with its cigar ash) and the prints of the hound. I generally have three sections of this course, so each one adds various elements to the crime scene throughout the day.

"The Musgrave Ritual" is unusual because it is a story within a story within a story, which obviously provides a good opportunity to discuss "frame stories." The action moves back and forth between the various time frames, so it can be a bit confusing. After reading the entire narrative, I have my students do the classic activity of putting the events in proper sequence—but because of the unusual structure of the story, the sequencing requires a good deal of thought and rereading of the text. As Holmes says, "What was the starting-point of this chain of events? There lay the end of this tangled line." Here is the activity:

Number the following events (1-14) in the correct chronological sequence:

3 _____ The Musgraves employ Brunton.

9 _____ Reginald Musgrave asks for Sherlock Holmes's assistance.

14 _____ Dr. Watson writes down the adventure of the Musgrave Ritual.

1 _____ Ralph Musgrave receives the valuables from Charles the Second.

4 _____ Brunton is caught in the library.

13 _____ Dr. Watson asks to hear about the Musgrave Ritual.

8 _____ Reginald Musgrave has the lake dragged.

9 _____ The Musgrave Ritual is invented.

5 _____ Rachel Howells traps Brunton in the cellar vault.

10 _____ Holmes figures out the meaning of the Ritual.

7 _____ Rachel Howells disappears.

6 _____ Brunton disappears.

12 _____ Watson asks Holmes to tidy up their apartment.

13 _____ Holmes tells Reginald Musgrave what he has really found in the lake.

I have only touched on a few activities that teachers can do with their students based on the work of Arthur Conan Doyle. ACD provides a rich vein, and I think both teacher and student will be well served by mining the writings of one of the most popular and prolific authors in the world. Using mysteries to engage students is, indeed, elementary.

VISUAL IMAGERY IN DISCUSSING LITERATURE
Barbara Szubinska, Eastern Kentucky University

The "eyes" have it!

Steeped in the simplicity of Hallmark cards and nursery rhymes, students have difficulties understanding literature, particularly poetry. Thus, when teaching poetry, I utilize an imagery-based technique. I make students engage their mind's eyes by illustrating the poems under discussion. This method allows students to visualize the content, and it allows me to make sure they pay attention to the details of the work under discussion. One of my favorite works to discuss in such a way is "The Love Song of J. Alfred Prufrock." Before analyzing the complexities of the poem, students listen to the author's reading of the poem and draw a set of illustrations that depict Eliot's descriptions of a city/London. For example, they make a drawing of the fog and smog compared to a cat. After discussing the setting of the poem and its historical context, students make caricatures of Prufrock based on individual lines from the poem, such as "I grow old...I grow old...I shall wear the bottoms of my trousers rolled." While students draw in groups (I allow approximately 10 minutes for drawing), I walk around the classroom and talk with them, pointing out good ideas as well as problems. For instance, they tend to draw Prufrock with a big happy, smiling face, which is not consistent with the person described in the poem. Therefore, illustrating makes students focus on the details of the poem. After the drawings are completed, we hang them up next to the pictures of London, and students present their caricatures and explain them. This activity makes students concentrate on the details of the work under discussion, it provides a visual accompaniment to the text, which helps them remember the scenes and images, and it helps set the stage for more in-depth discussion of the work during the following class.

WRITING

A SWIFT WAY TO SPARK INTEREST
Buffy Turner, Eastern Kentucky University

The race is to the swift.

I have found that the best way to spark interest in students who really don't seem to be very enthusiastic about English composition is through a lesson in literal and inferred meaning. I start out by giving them an in-class reading/ writing assignment. They are given a copy of Jonathan Swift's "A Modest Proposal" to read. For quite a few, this exposure is their first to Swift. The looks on their faces when they realize what he is proposing are priceless. The students actually have to question the proposal in their writing and tell me what they think Swift really meant—not what he said, but what he meant. They don't always get it right—some of their answers are even more amusing than the proposal itself—but it does make them seriously think about what they are reading. I usually follow this exercise up by making them write their own Swift-like proposal or use satire in a paper in order to get their point across.

REAL WRITIN'

John J. McKenna, University of Nebraska at Omaha

A "read-letter" day.

One of the most difficult problems facing a writing teacher is getting students to think of writing in the classroom as a rehearsal for their later-in-life, real-world communications. Throughout their 12 or more years of education, students write for the wrong audience. They write for the teacher. Oh, to be sure, the teacher is the only visible audience, and the teacher is "giving the grade." In focusing exclusively on the teacher as audience, however, the students never quite see that their writing will, someday, have an audience which operates on a very different social contract. I think that's why teachers feel the futility of their efforts, as they admonish their students to "consider your audience." Actually, the students have, and they've decided the teacher is their one and only audience.

What's wrong with this practice? Well, most communications within a classroom are not very similar to those in the real world. The students know that the teacher, most likely driven nearly to distraction by a crushing overload of work and trembling in fear of poor administrators and angry parents, will give any composition, however putrid, a passing grade. So, the students do the only logical thing—they hand in a putrid essay. It's certainly easier than writing a truly good essay, one that's a genuine and effective communication.

What's the answer? Well, part of it is to require students to submit their writing to an outside audience, someone other than the teacher. In my first-semester, freshman English classes, I require the students to write essays that originate in their own experience. This way they have something to bring to the table. The first essay assignment is to identify a problem from their own lives. The second essay proposes a solution to a problem. Part of the solution must include identifying a single, specific individual who could bring about or help effect a genuine solution. As a result, the students write about problems such as living in dorms, families too busy to get together for vacations, the difficulties of finding a church and reception hall for a wedding, lack of security at a neighborhood park, etc. All things they understand and know from direct experience.

During the last two weeks of the semester, the students look over all of their essays to select one for submission to an outside audience. In consultation with their peer editing group and me, they select, edit, revise, and improve this essay. Then, I teach them how to write an appropriate cover letter and address an envelope using a computer and printer. (You'd be surprised how many don't know how to execute this simple process.) But I don't trust them to send it! Not on their own.

On the last day of class, I supervise them as they get their essays, cover letters, and envelopes (with stamps) ready to take over to the university mail drop. Then, we go over as a class, and one by one the students drop their "real writin'" in the US Mail. Let me tell you: knowing they'll have to mail out an essay to somebody other than their beleaguered teacher puts a whole different spin on things. You can see that they take this process more seriously, and, as a result, do a much better job of writing. Give this approach a try. Your students will become more accomplished writers, if you make the process real. All it takes is a little dose of reality to get real writin'.

CLAD (CREATIVITY AND LANGUAGE APPRECIATION DAY)

Hal Blythe and Charlie Sweet, Eastern Kentucky University

Don't get mad, get CLAD.

We love words. We revel in their sound, their look, even their texture. We like olde words used in new contexts and new words used in old contexts. Of course, as kids we read a lot, but we also played around with words. Charlie remembers a nightly supper table game with his dad. During the day Charlie would look up a normal word that could be used in everyday conversation (no fair finding a bacteria common to New Zealand) and try to stump his dad. Hal recalls growing up in a family where bad puns were the norm. To this day Charlie has a vivid memory reading a comic book with the sentence "Steve Adams dons the famous outfit worn by Straight Arrow" and wondering what "dons" meant. Did Steve steal the clothes? Did he hit them with a tomahawk? Moments like this one required another trip to *Webster's*.

The longer we teach creative writing (and other writing courses as well), the more we realize that an absolute prerequisite for success as a writer is logophilia, the love of words. Somewhere John Updike said, "I've been called a doter on words. It's true." But just as long we've been told that "You can't teach talent/inspiration/creativity"(that is, you can't make people into Little John Updikes who are enamored with words). Maybe not, but we think a good instructor can and should nurture a love of words through a series of exercises, so here are some things you can get your students to try.

- Look up a new word in the dictionary.
- Write a sentence wherein its total number of words equals the numbers of letters in each word of the sentence.
- Provide a name/word/term that you heard in a recent movie/TV show/video/ chat room. If nothing registers, name any word that fascinates you.
- Tear the crossword puzzle out of a newspaper and see how much of it you can finish (hint: Monday's puzzles are usually the easiest).
- Make up a new word.
- e.e. cummings a word; that is, combine two words into one (e.g. "puddlewonderful"; our favorite coinage is a fraternity party being "Buddeliteful").
- Make a pun, bad or otherwise (e.g. a place for Internet conversation is a "chat womb").
- Come up with a new take on an old term (e.g. "First Place" might refer to either Eden or a womb).
- Make up a name for a bad student. What is it about the name that suggests the student isn't very good?
- Write a sentence wherein the first word and the last are the same.
- Write a sentence, and then write another that begins with the last word in the first sentence.

By the way, in our dictionary there's no such word as "logophilia," but so what?

SUPERCHARGING PROSE
Hal Blythe and Charlie Sweet, Eastern Kentucky University

You wouldn't take a Model T to the Spring Nationals Drags...

In an attempt to give their lectures more student appeal, several schools have actually hired writers to "punch up" classroom presentations, adding a joke here, dropping in an anecdote there, and perhaps providing "stage directions" for more effective delivery. How many times have you yearned for a consultant to punch up the prose you get from your students? Sure, their sentences are grammatically correct and their organization is solid, but the finished product just doesn't reach out and grab your attention, shouting, "Read me!"

Regardless of your discipline, several techniques exist to help your students supercharge their prose, making it more lively, more engaging — without sacrificing clarity or exactness.

1) **Employ Sentence variety.** Students tend to use the same sentence structures again and again since they feel comfortable with their correctness (We recently had a student write an essay containing nothing but compound sentences). Encourage students to vary their structures; after all, a semicolon serves the same purpose as a comma plus conjunction. Our language has four basic sentence structures (simple, compound, complex, and compound-complex), and the sophisticated writer uses them all.

2) **Avoid weak openers.** "There is," "There are," and "It is" delay the important material, relegating it to a subordinate position in the sentence. Consider the difference in effect between "There are several ways to help your students punch up their prose" and "Several ways exist to help your students punch up their prose." Weak openers not only dull effect, they constitute wasted words.

3) **Choose active verbs.** One of the best ways to breathe life into prose comes through using verbs that carry their own weight. Passive verbs (the "to be" gang) abdicate their power in favor of the nouns around them. Instead of "John was a good student in geography," try "John excelled in geography."

4) **Incorporate figurative language**. We are creatures of the senses, and, as a result, language that appeals to those senses often makes our point more forcefully. While many varieties of figurative language exist, the simile and metaphor provide perhaps the best avenues to enlivening your students' prose. To describe how something looks, sounds, tastes, or feels through reference to a more familiar "something" can constitute a powerful expressive tool. The simile (comparison) and the metaphor (identification) cause readers to encounter the subject on an other-than-mental plane. Instead of "I had a sour taste in my mouth," try "My mouth shriveled like the first time I bit into a green apple fresh picked from the tree"; instead of "She shouted shrilly," write "Her voice became a thousand fingernails running down a chalkboard."

5) **Select specific detail.** Nothing sterilizes a sentence more than generalities. As with figurative language, concrete detail brings life to prose. Further, generality allows for relativity; each reader may interpret the sentence according to individual experience or biases. What does the student mean by "big," "expensive," "pretty," or "smart"? Encourage students to replace such relative terms with concrete expression: "The building stood 25 stories tall" (big in Richmond, KY; not so big in Chicago); "She scored 1300 on the SAT" (smart for a regional college; perhaps not as "smart" in the Ivy League).

Don't let your students settle for horse-and-buggy prose when they can supercharge their essays with just a few changes.

TEACHING VOICE IN THE COMPOSITION CLASSROOM

Marshall Myers, Eastern Kentucky University

Use that tone of voice. . .please.

One of the most difficult concepts for composition students to understand in writing is "voice," that part of the writer's personality that seeps through the prose. Students find it nearly impossible to make inferences about the writer's persona as they read a passage, and, as a result, cannot discern how to inject the writer's voice into their own compositions.

I find that using the newspaper "personals" provides an understandable introduction to this concept. I ask students to try to visualize what type of person is speaking through the words the writer chooses. Does the writer reveal personality traits a reader may find attractive? Is the writer too forward? Does the writer mask qualities unattractive to the ad reader? In other words, what kind of personality comes through the words the writer chooses to attract a love partner?

I have discovered that students react quite easily and comfortably to the "personals" since, in many ways, they already have lots of experience trying to discern the "voice" of future mates.

I usually follow this exercise with samples of literary prose from writers who attempt to present a vivid personality in their work, voices like Huckleberry Finn, Ishmael, and Holden Caulfield. I, then, go on to techniques for creating voice in their own writing.

TEACHER AS WRITING ROLE MODEL

Claude Crum, Middle Tennessee State University

Don't close the door on your old drafts.

In my experience, the most useful technique for teaching writing is to be a writing role model for the students. Particularly in Freshman composition classes, it's not enough to simply review all the textbook writing processes and approaches to writing. It's hard to convince students to revise and edit their work, to do more than take the first draft hot off the printer and turn it in as a finished draft. They need proof that good writers actually do revise, rethink, reorganize.

That's where being a writing role model becomes important. I photocopy drafts of old essays, letters of submission, etc., anything I can find that I have written and revised and bring them to the class. Suddenly, I'm no longer the omnipotent entity who holds the key to the students' grades in the class. I've become a fallible human being and, more importantly, a fellow writer, a writer who occasionally misspells a word, forgets the comma with the coordinating conjunction between independent clauses, rearranges paragraphs within the essay, deletes or adds entire sentences or paragraphs as needed, and has to write several versions of the conclusion to get it just right. In short, I am a writing role model. I show them how each draft improves, from preliminary outline to final draft, and the students understand that writing is not so much an act as a process, a process with a series of steps, a series of steps that everyone, no matter how advanced, must complete.

PE

PROGRAM ADVOCACY
B. McKinley, Slippery Rock University

Just do it!

Many of my most effective assignments call on students to deal with real-world situations. The following calls on students to collaborate and react to a situation they might face in the career field using professional reference materials.

Background: During the first half of class tonight, we reviewed the National Association for Sport and Physical Education's (NASPE) position statement regarding the critical importance of continually being active advocates for daily physical education. In the "SPEAK II Sport and Physical Education Advocacy Kit," NASPE cited many blueprints for action to promote our discipline. As stated in the kit, "Even during a banner sales year, Nike keeps promoting every day the value of its products. The same approach needs to be taken with physical education."

"Your mission, should you choose to accept it…(If you choose not to accept this mission, your discipline will self-destruct in front of your eyes). . .is to respond to the attached letter from a Pennsylvania school district superintendent."

You will be working with a partner of your choice to formulate a well-designed advocacy response, using four of the following NASPE advocacy materials as references/guidelines:
1. "Is Your H/PE Program in Jeopardy?"
2. Top 10 Ways Physical Educators Can Be Better Program Advocates
3. A Report of the Surgeon General Physical Activity and Health At-a-Glance 1996 (Executive Summary)
4. What is Quality Physical Education?
5. The Shape of our Nation's Children
6. The Shape of the Nation Survey—1997 (Executive Summary)
7. Physical Activity and Sport in the Lives of Girls From The President's Council
8. Communicate, Educate!
9. Physical Education for Special Populations—NASPE

Be prepared to share your statement and substantiate your reply to the superintendent with the class.

November 21, 1993

Ronald Paranick, Principal
Franklin Area School District
RD #4 Box 325
Franklin, PA 16323

Dear Ron:

In regards to your request for information for grading physical education, I present the following thoughts. I believe Physical Education should be a pass/fail or satisfactory/unsatisfactory. If you must give a letter grade, remove it from use in class rank and honor roll computations.

Years ago, when I was high school principal, a male student who was an honor's student received A's and B's in every academic subject (advanced chemistry, math analyst, calculus, English, political science and physics). But he received C's in physical education. Henry was legally blind and overweight. Remarkably he could overcome his disability in academic areas, but was penalized because he could not physically.

I believe there is a difference between intellectual/cognitive development and achievement and physical development. We need to recognize the differences.

Sincerely,

MENDING THE FRACTURED PHYSICAL EDUCATION FAIRY TALE
B. McKinley, Slippery Rock University

Once upon a time . . .

Here's an assignment I use that involves students in critical thinking, creativity, composition—and it's fun.

Tonight in class, you and a partner of your choice will be reading "A Fractured Physical Education Fairy Tale." Your task is to re-write the story to correct any errors in teacher planning, class execution of teaching skills, and assessment of student learning. You may also want to address any program advocacy and safety issues that come to your attention. You are encouraged to construct your tale using "best practices" in physical education, National Association for Sports and Physical Education standards, and your knowledge of developmentally-appropriate, sequential activities. Have fun, and be prepared to share your work with the class! You will have 30 minutes to complete this assignment.

"A Fractured Physical Education Fairy Tale"

Once upon a time, in the Pretty City School District, Pat Perfect, the elementary school gym teacher, met Mrs. Hardwork's second grade class at the entrance to the gym. "Pat," said Mrs. Hardwork, "they're all yours! By the way, I kept Justin, Billy and Chastity in the room to work on their language arts assignment."

Pat greeted a couple of the boys with a feint to the right and a fake punch to the tummy, then placed the class in various stations. The class was divided into 6 groups: three groups of girls, and three of boys. The groups quickly got to work on the tasks. A number of students were thrilled that they were still playing four-square, after three weeks of class. Some of the children at the jump rope station were chasing each other, using their ropes as lassos. Pat spent most of the time at the far end of the room, working with three members of the 6th grade basketball team, since there was a big game after school that day, and it was important to add a win to the team record. The other basket was used as a shooting station, but the basketballs proved to be a bit heavy for the second graders.

Mrs. Maybe, the Principal, walked her class through the gym/cafeteria on their way to music class. Mrs. Maybe thought that the gym class was great; everyone was busy, they all looked happy, and the lesson looked like a good one.

A few times, Pat Perfect moved about the room. Pat was careful to offer clear instructions to the boys at the throwing and catching station, taking care to remind them to step with the opposite foot as they threw the ball and to be sure to follow through with their throwing arms. Pat also visited two of the girls' stations. At the rope jumping station, Pat praised Megan on her cute outfit and tweaked her curls. At the forward roll station, Pat urged Jill to try a little harder and concentrate really hard not to land on her head as she rolled forward.

Jacob, being his usual hyperactive self, was sent to sit on the edge of the stage, almost as soon as class began. He joined Ben, who was also there for a "time out" for complaining about having to play four-square during the previous class. Ben was relieved to only have to sit on the stage for two gym classes.

While working with the basketball players, Seth arrived at Pat's side, crying that he had fallen and hit his head on the cafeteria table lined up on the side wall. Pat told Seth to "shake it off" and sent him back to play.

At the end of class, Pat decided to skip the school board meeting that night since the basketball game wouldn't be over until dinner time. The board was considering program and staff cuts. Pat knew others would be there to represent the interests of the PE staff.

Mrs. Hardwork arrived to take the children back to class. Pat praised their deportment and hurried down to the teacher's lounge for lunch. Pat was anxious to complain to the other teachers about a couple of students who were being particularly difficult.

SCIENCE

MOLECULAR BIOGRAPHIES

Jessica L. Barker and Carl L. Aronson, Kettering University

I atom I cried . . .

In our freshman-level Industrial Organic Chemistry lecture course for engineering majors, we ask the students to submit several concise synopses of common organic molecules termed "Molecular Biographies." This novel exercise is primarily intended to introduce students to the chemicals that we depend on and use in everyday life. A secondary goal of this project is to give students experience at finding information about chemicals that they may be exposed to in their workplace or home environment. As an instructor, it is sometimes difficult to impress upon non-chemistry majors the importance and utility of chemistry beyond the classroom. With this assignment, students can see chemistry firsthand in an applied context and use this information to become informed engineers, citizens, and consumers. Many students have expressed their surprise upon learning what chemicals are contained in their everyday products and were certainly glad to learn how their medications work.

Students obtain the "subject" of their biographies by either selecting a molecule discussed in class, picking an ingredient from a favorite product's label, or choosing a pharmaceutical or polymer of interest. The type of molecular information that is required includes the common and systematic names, the structure, and how the molecule is used by society. Students are also encouraged to include information concerning the chemical's origin, commercial manufacturing process, biosynthesis, mode of action, and any unique properties or applications. Searches outside of the scientific literature can also uncover controversial issues regarding FDA approval, environmental concerns, or recycling issues. Intriguing examples of molecular biographies submitted to date include: propylene glycol, paclitaxel (Taxol), methylphenidate (Ritalin), cis-y-irone (violet scent in perfumes), polystyrene, polyethylene, and sodium benzoate.

Students at any school, regardless of their library's printed resources, can do this assignment as the majority of information can be obtained from the world wide web. Internet sites that students have found useful include: manufacturers' home pages; medical, academic, and government information sites; on-line encyclopedias; and public databases such as the United States Patent and Trademark Office. Students can also use conventional chemistry textbooks, encyclopedias, indexes, data handbooks, periodicals, and material safety data sheets.

OCCUPATIONAL THERAPY

HISTORICAL CONTRIBUTORS TO OCCUPATIONAL THERAPY
Kate Tuminski, Eastern Kentucky University

Who are those guys?

In preparation for teaching a class on the historical contributors to the Occupational Therapy profession, I give the students an article to read and a historical figure to research. The day of the class I divide the students into four groups of five. I give each group a marker and two transparencies. The first transparency is used to record each group member's research findings of the historical figure. The second transparency is used to record the group's perspectives of the impact of the historians on current and future practice. Each group then presents their findings to the remainder of the class. A discussion/lecture follows in which I discuss the article and how their research of historical figures validates what they read. I close the class by discussing the impact of the past on present and future occupational therapy service delivery. The activity is well received.

PAPER DOLLS
Kate Tuminski, Eastern Kentucky University

Playing dress-up . . . in the classroom

I teach a course in the Occupational Therapy curriculum entitled, "Therapeutic Activities." The course focus is the study of the value and use of activities in occupational therapy and the occupational performance skills in work, play/leisure and self care. One of the core concepts is for the student to understand his/her own values regarding activities, so I teach a session on culture. Following the lecture I give each of them a paper doll, markers, construction paper, and scissors. The students are then directed to dress the paper doll in their "favorite" clothing. (The activity allows them the opportunity for self expression which appears to be very important to them.) Following the activity students show the paper doll to classmates and discuss the relevance of the clothing to their cultural and personal preference. I gather the paper dolls and make a wreath with the dolls. The wreath then is posted on the room bulletin board as a reminder of the value of understanding a person's cultural similarities and differences.

MAKING THE PICTURE COMPLETE
Kate Tuminski, Eastern Kentucky University

A crafty approach

I teach a course in the Occupational Therapy curriculum entitled "Therapeutic Activities." The course focus is the study of the value and use of activities in Occupational Therapy and the occupational performance skills in work, play/leisure and self care. The first day of class I review the course content and then show the students a video entitled "A Story of Queen Anne's Lace." (Note: Before the video starts, I give each of the students a piece of dried Queen Anne's Lace as a sample representation of the type of flower in the video.) The video is a narrative by Dr. Steven Heater as he tells a powerful story of his interaction with an elderly patient in long-term care. He takes her outside to pick Queen Anne's Lace (a weed) in the field behind the nursing facility. The activity lasts over an hour, whereas previously the patient could not tolerate more than 5-10 minutes of activity without showing signs of fatigue. The activity was so meaningful to her that when Dr. Heater escorted her back to her room, she said, "Sorry we did not get to do therapy today," little realizing she had more occupational therapy than she had experienced in many months.

After viewing the video, students are then given a picture frame, construction paper, glue, scissors, and a piece of Saran wrap. They secure the flower on the construction paper. Students can use individual self expression to decorate the frame but must include the phrase "Occupational Therapy is …" They then glue on the frame and cover the entire picture with Saran wrap. I suggest they take the project home and pin it to a bulletin board as a sample representation of the value of purposeful activities used by the Occupational Therapy profession in providing direct service to patients. Thus begins the process of developing a professional identity.

LIBRARY

WHERE IN THE LIBRARY. . .
Julie George, Eastern Kentucky University

Where in the world is . . .

Amount of time required:
8-10 minutes

Purpose:
What do you hope the students will gain from this technique? To familiarize the students with locations inside the library and to give them a fun-filled approach (vs. merely handing them a map).

Class:
What class and level did you use the technique with or would you recommend it for? I have used this technique in GSO classes of many levels, ENG 101 and ENG 102, and ACS 101 (intro to business). I would recommend it for any class that may have students who are unfamiliar with the library.

Materials:
- Colored markers, one for each student (not necessary but it makes it fun)
- 8 1/2 x 11 pieces of colored paper, one for each student (can be white, but colored is more exciting)
- Flip chart or white board and markers for either

Procedure:
- Pass out a marker and piece of colored paper to each student.
- Inform students that they are going to be drawing a map of the library to help them learn where areas are located.
- Have the students draw four lines on the paper to represent each floor of the library. The librarian draws four lines on the white board as well. The four lines should take up the entire piece of paper.
- Have students number each line 1 to 4 with 1 being the bottom line and 4 being the top line.
- Ask students on what floor the entrance is located. When they answer the second floor, draw a little set of doors on the line representing the second

floor. Explain that this can be confusing because you enter the building on the second floor, not the first.

- Now direct their attention to the first floor and ask if anyone knows what is on the first floor. When they say something like magazines or newspapers, explain it is the periodicals department and draw a little magazine on the first floor to represent that department (silly icons aid memory).

- Ask if there is anything else on the first floor. They will sometimes say things like videos (instructional media) and classrooms (108 for example). Don't draw these. Acknowledge their answers, but wait to see if the students mention the Archives or Special Collections. If they don't come up with this information, then tell them, write "Special Collections" on the first floor and give a quick explanation about what it is.

- Move on to the second floor. In the end, the map should include the reference desk, circulation desk, grand reading room, and maybe the 24 x 7 lab and info desk. Draw a picture of a desk with a little person behind it for the reference desk and a bigger desk with more people behind it for the circulation desk. For the grand reading room, you can just abbreviate it as GRR and explain that this is where the popular reading collection is located and that they can get books there that are not exactly academic or they can find books to just browse through.

- Move on to the third floor. The map should include LRC, gov docs, law library, and the beginning of the stacks A-D. For the LRC draw a little apple and explain what is available in the LRC. Sometimes it helps to ask if there are any students in the class who are education majors. Explain what Government Documents is and abbreviate it "Gov Docs." Mention the law library and just write "law." Then draw a small bookshelf and write A-D on it and explain it is the beginning of the stacks.

- Move on to the fourth floor and draw a big bookshelf and write E-Z on it and explain it is the continuation of the rest of the stacks. Also mention that this floor is the quiet study floor and then draw a SHHHHHH on that floor. At this point ask the class if anyone has checked out a wireless laptop. Explain that they can check out a laptop from the circ desk and take it anywhere in the library to study, surf the web, check email, write papers, etc.

- Also mention that the library has two remote locations. Mention the Music Library. Draw a box and write a musical note in it with "Foster Bldg" near it. Mention the Justice and Safety Library and draw a box and write "Stratton" next to it.

- The map is now complete. Remind the students to keep this map and that it will help them in the future when they are trying to locate library materials.

Obviously, this exercise is EKU-specific, but could be adapted to any library/large building.

WHAT DON'T YOU LIKE?
Julie George, Eastern Kentucky University

So what's not to like?

Amount of time required:
7 minutes

Purpose:
What do you hope the students will gain from this technique? To disprove student stereotypes, beliefs, or assumptions about the EKU Library and its services.

Class:
I have used this technique in almost every class I have instructed.

Materials:
Index cards cut in half, one for each student (can be scrap paper).

Procedure:
- Pass out the cards.
- Ask the question: "What do you dislike about the library?"
- Give the students about 2-3 minutes to answer the question.
- Collect the cards.
- Glance through the cards as you collect them.
- Explain that this activity is being done to help the students learn about the library.
- Read the reasons why the students don't like the library out loud. (You can skip duplicate answers.)
- After each "dislike," try to find a way to make it positive. For example:

    Student writes: Library is confusing
    Librarian says: "Yes, the library is very confusing, but after this class period you will have a much better understanding of where materials are located and how to find them."

Student writes: Too far of a walk from my dorm/apartment

Librarian says: "Yes, the walk can be long, but I am going to show you how to access a great deal of information over the web. So, if you have a computer with Internet access, sometimes you can complete your research without ever leaving your room."

Student writes: Can't find anyone to help me

Librarian says: "Yes, sometimes it seems like all of the employees are busy, but did you know that there are actually seven reference librarians whose main job responsibility is to help you, the student? We are always at the reference desk until 9:30 in the evenings and all weekend. Sometimes you may have to wait a minute, but it is our job to help you. There are also desks throughout the building that are staffed with employees to help you."

KEYWORD CONNECTION
Kari Lyons, Eastern Kentucky University

The swami of origami

In order to effectively complete assignments, students often need to search electronic databases and resources to find information on a particular topic. Unfortunately, getting started with research can often overwhelm and confuse students. To ensure they are prepared with the tools necessary to begin the research process, the instructor should help the student understand and use keyword searching effectively.

The purpose of the activity is to:
* Help students develop a list of keywords for their topic
* Ensure each student has a list of keyword search statements they can use in their research
* Encourage interaction between students and their peers

To complete the Keyword Connection, each student will need a piece of paper and pen or pencil (although colored paper and markers add a nice twist to the activity).
1. Have the students fold their paper into three panels like a brochure.
2. Have them write their topic at the top of the middle column and write the word "Keywords" at the top of the 1st and 3rd columns.

3. Discuss the purpose of keywords, including their significance, examples of keywords, and reasons they benefit the student.
4. Have each student pass the paper to his or her neighbor, look at their neighbor's topic, and make a list of appropriate keywords on the 1ˢᵗ (or left side) panel of the paper.
5. After 1-2 minutes, have the student fold the 1ˢᵗ panel over to hide the list of words and hand the paper back to the original student. Encourage the original owners not to sneak any peeks at the hidden list.
6. Have the original student take 1-2 minutes to make his or her own list of keywords on the 3ʳᵈ (or right side) panel of the paper.
7. Demonstrate how an effective keyword search statement should be created using Boolean operators, parentheses, and quotation marks.
8. Have the students unfold their papers and read both lists of keywords. Using the center panel of the paper, have each student create keyword search statements using the keywords listed.
9. If electronic resources are available, have students practice using their search statements. If the resources are not available, assure students they now have the necessary tools to begin their research and encourage them to try using their search statements as soon as possible.

BOOLEAN BASICS
Kari Lyons, Eastern Kentucky University

Boola, boola …

To teach the "Boolean Basics," or basics of using Boolean operators in creating effective search statements, you'll need a deck of normal playing cards and a classroom full of student participants. Begin the activity by defining the purpose of keywords and keyword searching. Progress into a brief discussion of Boolean operators (AND, OR, and NOT) and explain how they are used to broaden and narrow search results. After the discussion, conduct the following exercise:
1. Give every student a playing card (not including Jokers).
2. Ask all students with BLACK cards to stand. Count the number of standing students and write it on the board.
3. Ask all students with BLACK AND FACE cards to stand. Count the number of standing students, write it on the board with the word AND, and ask the students what changed with the results (results should increase).

4. Next, ask all students with BLACK OR FACE cards to stand. Count the number of standing students, write it on the board with the word OR, and ask the students what changed with these results (results should increase yet again).

5. Finally, have only students with (BLACK OR FACE) NOT KINGS stand. Count the number of standing students, write it on the board with the word NOT, and ask one last time what changed with the search results (results should decrease).

Talk with students about how they, like the example, can broaden or narrow their searches by effectively using Boolean operators in their search statements.

CUT-ACROSS

FRAMING RESEARCH
Judith Heady, University of Michigan-Dearborn

Questions, questions everywhere.

In my upper-level embryology class, I use articles from current literature in the field as the primary "texts." Students come prepared to discuss and present the research in the articles based on a framework that asks questions, such as "What is the purpose of this research? What are the experimental and control groups? What did they do step by step in outline form?" and on to "What are the basic embryology concepts related to this work?" There are usually two articles for each session, and half the class reads each one and presents that at the board for the other half (front and back blackboards). I keep notes on both and file them for reference. Students take open-notes examinations that are essentially in-class essays in which they utilize discussions of methods, results, and concepts to answer questions based on the presentations. They have detailed rubrics so that they can plan generally for what they will write.

I use this testing technique in a number of my classes where the topics are studied from current literature. The in-class open-book/open-notes format allows students to explain with some detail complicated arguments supported by the actual explanations of the research steps. They must choose and connect good examples of experiments/papers to the topic(s) asked for. I find that explaining in this fashion allows me to judge how well they actually understand the techniques and the concepts. I have used this in Embryology, Women's Health, Gender and Science, and for part of each examination in Discoveries in Current Biology, a graduate course for teachers in a Master's degree program in Education.

UNIFORM TERMINOLOGY *JEOPARDY*
Kate Tuminski, Eastern Kentucky University

It's all in the game.

One of the techniques I use in the classroom that students find helpful and fun is to play "Uniform Terminology Jeopardy" with key terms and concepts they need to learn related to specific uniform terminology of the Occupational Therapy profession. I have a class of 14 or 15 students, and I divide them into 3 teams of 5 students to compete against one another. Their prizes in the past have been everything from 10 extra bonus points for the semester's grade to pieces of my button jewelry to $1.00 coupons from McDonald's. I use this strategy just before a test as a means of reviewing the content from the unit being covered in the exam. Their test scores seem to reflect the benefit of the activity. I have had several students thank me for the opportunity to play the game as it did one of two things: (1) It reminded them that they had more studying to do, or (2) They really had retained the information necessary to do well on the test. The competition between them is interesting to watch, and they seem to actively engage in the learning process. (I, too, have a lot of fun!)

ALMOST *JEOPARDY*
Regina Galer, Purdue University

I'll take "Success" for $200, Alex.

Every now and then, I stop the action of the class and play "Almost Jeopardy." This exercise is a highly modified version of the popular game show which I use in some of the courses that I teach. It is a particularly effective form of review for an intensive, cumulative final exam. I use it as a review of the course material, and I find that the game show format refreshes students' memory, decreases anxiety, and increases test performance. Here's how we play:

Students are asked to review for the test using the review sheet that has been given to them one week prior to the Jeopardy session. Upon arriving at class, I appoint the top student in the class to help me with scoring, and I break the rest of the group into three teams. In large classes, the teams are very large, but it doesn't matter. Prior to class, I have assembled questions (some are exam questions from previous semesters) on 3x5 cards. Sometimes I have each student bring 2-3 questions and answers written on index cards. I read the questions, and we play team Jeopardy. My student helper watches for the first hand to go up and aids me in the score keeping process. The student helper also helps me to distribute small prizes that help to maintain student interest. "Corny" answers get a can of corn, an individual who is "hogging" the floor gets a can of SPAM (cheaper than a canned ham), and good answers might merit a pen, pencil, or magnet that I have procured at a recent conference. After Final Jeopardy, we rank order the teams. The losers get hard candy, the middle team gets a Hershey's kiss, and the winners receive a very small candy bar.

What did we accomplish? A very fun, but useful, review session has just taken place. Many students have told me that the session motivated them to study harder for the exam because they felt they had a good jump on studying, they felt more at ease with the material, and they believed they could perform well on this exam. The benefit to the students and to your rapport with the students far outweighs the small amount spent on prizes.

GAME SHOWS IN THE CLASSROOM
Andrea Peach, Georgetown College

Tonight on the Game Show Channel

I use a variety of games in my classes. For example, I have a Power Point version of "Jeopardy" which teaches basic computer hardware. I use this in my Classroom Applications of Technology course to review/discuss hardware, to illustrate this special use of Power Point, and to teach about using games for teaching. The students love it! I also use a Word version of "Hollywood Squares" in a similar manner, and have even created "Who Wants to be a Millionaire" for reviewing concepts. A colleague of mine in Chemistry also uses the "Millionaire" game for her class. I sometimes give prizes (candy bars) to the winners.

FUN TEAM-BUILDING ACTIVITIES
Heather Hall, Elmhurst College

Oh, the games people play now.

INITIALIZERS

LOOK TAG
Materials Needed: None
Activity: Divide participants into two groups. Have each group form a circle approximately 20 feet away from one another. Each group member bends over with their head down and their hands on their knees. At the count of three the facilitator yells out the word "look." Each participant quickly looks up at another person in their group. If that person is staring back at them, both individuals must run to the other group's circle. If an individual looks up and no one is looking at them, they bend over with their hands on their knees and wait for the facilitator to give the "look" command again. *Variation: After a few minutes, have group members make a silly face as they look up.

BALLOON RACE
Materials Needed: Balloons
Activity: Divide participants into groups of 5 or 6, giving each person a balloon. Have each team form a single file line on an end line. At the command "go," the first person in each line blows up their balloon and then releases it. The entire group must run to the point where the first balloon lands and must line up behind the balloon with the second person in line moving up and repeating the process. This procedure is continued until the entire team gets to the designated finish point. At that time the whole team must blow their balloons up and play a recognizable tune in order to finish. The facilitator should be ready to hand out extra balloons in case of breakage.

ALASKAN BASEBALL
Materials Needed: Plastic baseball bat and a Whiffle or Nerf ball
Activity: Divide group members into two teams. One team is in the outfield; the other team is up to bat. The pitcher pitches and the batter swings to hit the ball (there are no foul balls and the "one strike and you're out" rule applies). If the ball is hit, the batter runs around his/her team as many times as possible with each complete lap counting as a run. In the meantime, the fielding team runs to

the person on their team who fielded the ball and must line up in a straight line behind that person. Once all members of the fielding team form a line behind the fielder, the batting team can no longer score runs. After three outs the teams switch. Play 3-4 innings. Facilitators should keep track of legal runs. Partial laps do not count as a run. *Variation: Fielding team must pass the ball over and under to the end of their line in order for the "at bat" to be complete.

HOOP RACE
Materials Needed: 6-8 large hula hoops
Activity: Place 8-10 people on a team and have each team line up in a straight line facing you. Each group should hold hands by reaching backward through their legs and grabbing the free hand of the person behind them. Each team requires a starter. The starter is given 3-4 hula hoops. At the signal to begin, the starter places a hoop over the head of the first person in line. As soon as the hoop reaches the third person in line, the starter adds another hoop. This continues until the starter has run out of hoops. At this time, the starter becomes the first person in line. Once all of the hoops reach the last person in line, that person brings the hoops to the front of the group and the process begins again. The race continues until the original front person returns to that spot.

COMMUNICATION ACTIVITIES

THE MAZE
Materials Needed: Balls, cones, jump ropes, 150' rope, blindfolds, a hula hoop, and any other available objects
Activity: Take the 150' rope and make a large circle with it. Put the hula hoop in the center of the circle. Then take all of your objects and make a maze within the circle. Have group members partner up. One partner is blindfolded and the other partner remains sighted. The sighted partner leads, by hand, the blindfolded partner to the edge of the maze. The sighted partner then goes to the opposite side of the maze, and by giving only verbal commands, leads the blindfolded partner through the maze. The blindfolded partner must get into the hula hoop and back out of the maze without touching any of the objects. Should a touch occur, the sighted partner goes to their partner, physically leads them out of the maze, and begins again. After successfully completing the maze, the partners switch roles. No cheating should be tolerated!

WHAT'S THAT SPELL?
Materials Needed: Phrases written on pieces of paper
Activity: Divide your group in half. Using their bodies as letters, one group

tries to spell out phrases that you have written on pieces of paper. The other group tries to figure out what they are spelling. Switch roles after two or three phrases.

LOW LEVEL ACTIVITIES

LOG OFF
Materials Needed: 1 log 12' long or one 12'2" x 6" plank
Activity: Have group members number off 1-6, 1-8, or 1-10 and have them stand on the log. Without falling off the log, 1 must get to where 10 is, 10 must get to where 1 is, 2 must get to where 9 is, 9 must get to where 2 is, etc. If anyone falls off of the log, all group members must return to their original positions and begin again.

HIGH LEVEL ACTIVITIES

SPIDER WEB
Material Needed: Two 8' (2" x 4"), two 12' (2" x 4"), elastic or string, eye hooks, eight 4" carriage bolts, eight nuts, and 16 washers
Activity: Create a spider web with the materials listed above. Attach the finished web to a volleyball standard or something sturdy so that it will not fall. Place padded mats on each side of the web. Each member of the group must get through the web without touching any part of it. Once a hole is used, it cannot be used again. If the web or frame is touched by any part of the body, clothing, or hair, the group must start over from the beginning. At this time, all of the holes may be used again. Try to make the web look different each time you do this challenge. If you have 10 people, make sure you have at least 11 usable holes, if you have 8 people, have at least 9 usable holes, etc.

ELECTRIC FENCE
Materials Needed: High jump standards, a high jump bar, and padded mats
Activity: The object is to get all group members over the fence without having anyone's clothing or body touch the fence. If anyone touches, the entire group must start over. Once over the fence, a group member may not go back to the other side to help other members of the group. The facilitator must spot the first and last person over the bar. The facilitator must also make sure that the group does not do anything to endanger the safety of a group member. The height of the bar should be no higher than the chest of the shortest person in the group.

PARTNER PROJECTS
Wallace R. Wood, University of Cincinnati

Swing your partner...

After having divided the class into teams, I go one step further and tell my students the following:

Partner Projects require a partner not in one's assigned Team. The very nature of this experience requires two people doing each task together. Partners from different number teams will have separately learned the various skills of the assignment and will have alternative peer groups for progress feedback.

Partners for Projects must find each other and find a client by the quarter's drop day. The Client firm can be any business where you are not currently an employee or in management. If you do not find a partner and a client company, Dr. Wood will sign and process the "W" drop slip to avoid the inevitable "I" or "F" due to students starting too late on projects.

Partner Projects will involve interview, documentation, and internal control analysis on local business. The project is graded on following directions. Projects are due the last class meeting before the final. Late projects receive the "I" for incomplete if and only if a written request for that grade is received on the project deadline. The I-request must include when the project will be completed and must include partners' mailing addresses.

All projects are returned at the Final Exam. Professor Wood has no storage space to keep unreturned projects and cannot make other students' work available for you to see without written permission of those past students anyway. Client firms can be most any business or even not-for-profit enterprise but do not attempt to work for my class at your current part-time employer. It will be too easy to look like you are doing your homework while on the time clock. If your co-op job is in public accounting, please be very sensitive to approaching a former client of your accounting employer. It might look like expensive audit work when you do your project and our workpapers could be confused for public accounting workpapers.

For a small business control analysis will be for both revenue and expense cycles and small is defined by maintaining only one checking account. Larger firms call for either revenue or expense cycle control analysis—choose expense if the firm sells face-to-face without billing credit sales.

For a partner, choose another student who can be relied on to tell you the truth and will do their fair share of competent work. Once you have become partners you are stuck together and neither is free to drop the course without taking a "WF." As the song suggests: "Better shop around."

DOCUMENTING SOURCES
Barbara Szubinska, Eastern Kentucky University

The system is the solution.

The lesson on documenting sources looms over the students and the instructors alike. Students consider it an unnecessarily complex, artificial construct in addition to all the other complexities involved in composing a research paper. Instructors are seldom enthusiastic about the topic because students are not willing to attend to the minutia of the task. Composition textbooks exacerbate the problem since they present documenting sources as a series of examples of individual citations, thus creating an impression of incoherence.

The table on page 89 helps me present documenting sources as a system. In addition to the traditional models of individual citations, the table arrangement focuses on the similarities among the citations instead of the differences. For example, I point out to the students that regardless of what source we are documenting, we try to identify its author(s) and put that information first; then, we look for the title and decide if the source is an independent one, which will appear underlined, or a part of a larger entity, which will appear in quotation marks. Students can see that the order in which information is presented in citations as well as the conventions for identifying titles are the same for all sources. This method, that focuses on documenting sources as a system, allows students not only to compose citations with confidence, but it also allows them to successfully negotiate citations in the sources they are reading.

Worksheet for Documenting the Most Commonly Used Sources in MLA Style

*Pay close attention to punctuation.   * If any information is not available, just move to the next part.   *Shaded boxes do not need to be filled.

	Author. Last name, first name		Title of the Book.	Editor. (If any)	City:	Publisher,	Year.	
Book	Author. Last name, first name		Title of the Book.	Editor. (If any)	City:	Publisher,	Year.	
Example	Kingsolver, Barbara.		The Bean Trees.		New York:	HarperPerennial,	1988.	
Your Example								
Work in a Collection	Author.	"Title of the Essay or Story."	Title of the Book.	Editor's name. (If any)	City:	Publisher,	Year.	
Example	O'Connor, Flannery.	"The King of the Birds."	The Bedford Reader.	Ed. X.J. Kennedy and Dorothy Kennedy.	New York:	St. Martin's Press,	1988.	
Your Example								
Article or Essay in a Magazine	Author.	"Title of the Article."	Title of the Magazine (no period)				Day Month Year:	pages.
Example	Ali, Lorraine.	"ASame Old Song."	Newsweek				9 Oct. 2000:	31-49.
Your Example								
Entry in a Reference Book	Author. (If any)	"Title of the Entry."	Title of the Reference Book,	Edition Number. (If any)			year.	

BLACKBOARD USE
Gene Kleppinger, Eastern Kentucky University

Blackboard … it's not a jungle out there.

My number 1 tip would be "Get a Blackboard site for your class!" With a Blackboard site you give yourself easy email access to your students, the capability to keep discussions going outside class hours, an online gradebook, etc. and etc.

Blackboard course sites are available for anyone, anywhere. If your campus doesn't offer Blackboard or an equivalent such as WebCT, you can always use the free service of Blackboard.com.

SPONGEBOB SQUAREPANTS LIVES
Hal Blythe and Charlie Sweet, Eastern Kentucky University

Please don't send in the clones.

Here's a little exercise that you can try the first day. Walk into the classroom, say a few words about class and your expectations, and then introduce yourself as Professor SpongeBob SquarePants or some equally ridiculous name.

First, you'll get a laugh, which is always good for the ego and at relieving pre-course tension. Second, you can make some points. If your students are like most, they've opened their notebooks and are faithfully copying in everything you say. Point out that while success in your course necessitates taking basic notes, they need not copy down everything you say verbatim so that they can exactly reproduce it on tests. Emphasize you want them not just taking notes, but thinking about what you are telling them (as they doubtless did when you gave them your wacky name). Lastly, stress that what you most assuredly don't want out of this class is Little SpongeBobs, that you have enough children, and that you did not ask the registrar to send in the clones to your class (this last point is very important in artistic classes wherein you don't want them imitating everything you create).

Something little, something memorable, something effective.

PERFORMANCE APPRAISAL PROVIDING FEEDBACK

Laura Koppes, Eastern Kentucky University

The play's the thing.

Objective: The objective of this activity is to provide students an opportunity to practice guidelines for giving positive and constructive feedback. Students also experience a training technique, role-playing, used in industry.

Method: The students are assigned to pairs. As a class, we review guidelines for providing positive and constructive feedback in a work setting. The students role-play various scenarios; one student plays the role of an employee and the other student plays the role of a supervisor. Examples are below.

Positive Feedback

"Jane has completed tabulating the results of a study two days ahead of schedule. This already completed work will allow you to prepare a set of comparative figures in time for your staff meeting. Give positive feedback to Jane."

Constructive Feedback

"Ted has just completed a report for a special project three days ahead of schedule. While reading through the report, you find that he did not include essential information from two departments. Give corrective feedback to Ted."

MOTIVATION IN THE WORKPLACE: GOAL SETTING

Laura Koppes, Eastern Kentucky University

Goal mining …

Objective: The objective of this activity is to help students learn and understand a theory of work motivation, goal setting theory. The students apply the theory to learning in the course.

Method:
Step 1: During the 2nd week of class, the students develop specific, chal-

lenging but attainable goals for the course. In addition, they specify what they will do to accomplish the goals and identify any possible obstacles.

Step 2: During mid-semester (7th week), I give each student a mid-semester progress report (feedback on the goals). They then compare the report with the goals they established in Step 1. They review each goal (and sometimes reset it) and determine the appropriate steps to accomplish the goal(s) by the end of the semester.

Step 3: During the last week of the semester, I give the students a progress report, which they compare to the goals they reviewed in Step 2. I ask them to reflect upon their goals and to explain their progress or lack of progress.

WHO IS A LEADER? WHY?
Laura Koppes, Eastern Kentucky University

What's My Line?

Objective: The objective of this activity is to help students understand the different theories of leadership.

Method:
Students are assigned to small groups of three individuals. Each group is assigned a theory of leadership. Their task is to describe a leader using the specific theory (e.g., trait theory, behavioral theory, situational theory). The students are asked to not use any language of the theory. The group then describes the individual to the entire class. The class determines the theory.

CONNECTING EXPERIENCE AND CONCEPT
Douglas Reimondo Robertson, Eastern Kentucky University

Growth Rings

The following procedure illustrates the use of several inter-related learning cycles (generating a concrete experience through recall, reflecting on it, forming abstract conceptualizations from it, and trying out these conceptualizations in the context of discussion). The course topic is adult development, and this exercise occurs at the beginning of the course as a prelude to beginning an exploration of pertinent theory and research. For a number of years, the process below has consistently produced the following results: (a) the anchoring of the discussion of adult development theory and research in the personal experience of participants, (b) the introduction of the course's key concepts, and (c) the illustration of how to learn from experience. The process has been adapted to other subject areas.

Individuals. Within the context of the large group, ask individual participants to brainstorm times in their lives when they felt that they had grown—become a different and better person. Ask them to list as many episodes as they can without editing. After about a minute, request that they select one of these significant periods to re-experience. Participants need to know that they will re-visit these life episodes because some of the growth episodes may have traumatic elements that individuals do not want to re-live within the class context. Once everyone has selected a growth experience, then proceed.

Individuals. Again, within the context of the large group, guide a visualization of these growth experiences. Explain that students are free to choose not to participate in this visualization exercise, and that if they make this choice, they must avoid disturbing other students. Usually, everyone chooses to participate. Ask students to place both of their feet on the floor, to put their hands on their thighs or in their laps, to sit up straight, and to close their eyes. Ask them to concentrate on their breathing—slowly, deeply, in and out, breathing in calmness and relaxation and breathing out the tensions of the day. If time allows, relax students' whole bodies, beginning with their feet and working up through the body to the head. Remind them periodically to breathe. Once they are in a relaxed state, ask students to visualize themselves during the period of their lives that they chose to re-experience. Invite them to let their minds roam free through events, especially trying to sense how they changed and people around them changed as they went through their growthful transitions. What were they thinking? How did they feel? What did they do? What did people with whom they had relationships think, feel, and do? What changed from beginning and middle to the end? Remind them to breathe periodically. After sufficient time to re-experience the events, tell students that they are going to leave that time and come back to this classroom, here and now. Ask them to breathe out that time and to breathe in this time. Suggest that when they open their eyes they will feel refreshed. Instruct them to open their eyes as they feel ready. As people are opening their eyes, instruct participants to brainstorm as many features of that growth experience as they can. What stands out to them about that experience? How had they changed? What were the features of the beginning, middle, and end? Again, ask them not to edit, but to brainstorm. As the brainstorm appears to be over, ask them to review their lists of characteristics and to star the most important ones.

Small groups. In groups of four (or larger if necessary), ask participants to describe briefly their growth experiences and to share their lists of its major features. The group's tasks are as follows: (a) to select someone who will report to the large group, (b) to identify the features of their growth experiences that are shared in common, and (c) to delineate any major differences among the experiences of the group members.

Large group. Each of the groups report. The teacher charts the lists of common characteristics from each group. The task of the large group is to identify commonalities among the groups. The level of abstraction—and robustness—grows from individual to the small group to the large group and eventually to the scholarly literature. The teacher makes the link to the literature, pointing out that the students' experience has yielded many, if not most, of the prominent concepts and findings from the adult development literature. Normally, students understand deeply how the ideas that they are about to read are really just expressions of their own lives.

AFTERWORD

Recently we participated in a campus-wide forum on assessing teaching. When we shared a list of traits our department had identified as belonging to good teachers, a young professor from a different department objected, saying he thought the list was severely limiting, might not even cover his style of teaching, and smacked of Big Brother in the classroom. Our response was that a list of good traits ought to be broad enough to include many different pedagogies and that all effective pedagogies share many similar traits. Far from being exclusive, such a list, we argued, needs to be inclusive.

In truth, in our many years of teaching, mentoring, and researching, we have encountered numerous pedagogical perspectives, policies, and practices. While many effective teachers exist, no two classroom experiences are the same. We have, however, discovered what we believe to be a core of behaviors that unite outstanding teachers regardless of school or discipline.

So, in the spirit of *USA Today* minimalism, we present:

TEN TIMELY TIPS FOR TERRIFIC TEACHING, or The Pedagogue's Decalogue.

1. Establish rapport, mutual respect, and high expectations with your students.
2. Arrive at class early and stay around at the session's end.
3. Clearly delineate the class session's beginning and end by previewing what is to come and reviewing the main points that emerged.
4. Give each class session context by placing it in the continuum of sessions that came before and those that will follow (know your material; don't be just minutes ahead of your students).
5. Be open and honest with students; be willing to admit that you screwed up or that you don't know something, but will get back to them next class about it.
6. Be consistent, especially in grading.
7. Use relevant illustrations and examples, especially when the session seems abstract.

8. Make all materials (syllabus, assignments, exams) clear and precise (e.g. instead of saying, "Read Chapter XII," try, "Read Chapter XII to discover the major factors in the emergence of Realism."

9. Return assignments (exercises, tests, papers) promptly with clear markings throughout the paper.

10. Be enthusiastic so that your students will enjoy the material as much as you do (which means you must love what you do and stay open to new approaches to the subject and pedagogy).